T0339294

Praise for

Liturgies for Hope

"It's hard to put into words just how much this book means to me. I found these prayers (or perhaps they found me) at the time I needed them the most. Like the friends of the poor soul who lay crippled on his mat, they have faithfully and delicately carried me, cared for me, and lowered me into the presence of the Healer.

"Audrey and Elizabeth have done incredible work here; they have spoken into the chaos with words of peace, poetically crafted and pastorally given. I am so grateful for these prayers."

—JOSHUA LUKE SMITH, poet, pastor, and
author of *Something You Once Knew*

"As someone who has spent many hours praying, here's what I've come to realize: it's still very hard to do. One of the best gifts that has helped me develop my life with God is the prayers and liturgies of others. I often need the words of others to help me form my own words. This is what Audrey Elledge and Elizabeth Moore do for us in this needed book. They offer beautiful words to help us access the longings of our souls and bring them to God. If you're looking for a jumpstart to your spiritual life, start here."

—RICH VILLODAS, lead pastor of New Life Fellowship
and author of *Good and Beautiful and Kind*

"This is a marvelous book. I am not surprised it emerged from one of the urban epicenters of our global pandemic—of course this fierce hope would grow in such a place and such a season. Audrey Elledge and Elizabeth Moore weave rich Scriptural imagery into powerful, prayerful poetry covering topics that are at once universal but also timely in their particularity. The liturgical pronouns shift between *we, you,* and *I* in a way that is spacious and welcoming. Best of all, this book compelled even this solitary reader to reach out to her friends; these are liturgies that simply must be prayed in the company of others."

—CHRISTIE PURIFOY, author of *Placemaker*

"*Liturgies for Hope* will be a trusted companion for those who struggle to find words for the cry of their hearts. In this book, Audrey and Elizabeth encourage us to lay our deepest requests before the Lord as a humble act of worship. This collection of prayers stirred my heart's affection for Christ by reminding me of the strong hope we have in Him."

—HUNTER BELESS, founder and host of the *Journeywomen* podcast and author of *Read It, See It, Say It, Sing It!*

Liturgies for Hope

FOREWORDS BY
JON TYSON AND PETE HUGHES

Liturgies for Hope

Sixty Prayers for the Highs, the Lows, and Everything in Between

**AUDREY ELLEDGE
AND ELIZABETH MOORE**

FORM

First published in the USA in 2022 by WaterBrook,
an imprint of Random House, a division of Penguin Random House LLC

First published in Great Britain in 2022

Form
36 Causton Street
London SW1P 4ST
www.spck.org.uk

Book design by Elizabeth A. D. Eno

British Library Cataloguing-in-Publication Data
A catalogue record for this book is available from the British Library

ISBN 978–0–281–08765–5
eBook ISBN 978–0–281–08766–2

3 5 7 9 10 8 6 4 2

First printed in Great Britain by Clays Ltd

Produced on paper from sustainable sources

For our families, both given and chosen,
who cultivated in us the gifts of poetry
and prayer

Contents

CONTENTS

CONTENTS

CONTENTS

Foreword by Pete Hughes

In a beautiful interview on the significance of the Psalms, Bono, the lead singer of U2, encourages Christian artists to create art that encompasses the full spectrum of the human experience: the agony as well as the ecstasy, the moments of desolation as well as the moments of triumph. He laments that much of Christian music and art fits within a narrow bandwidth between the two, unable to touch and speak into the extremities of our human experience. His rallying cry is that we need Spirit-inspired art that helps us to bring the whole of our lives into conversation and communion with God.

Liturgies for Hope is a beautiful example of this. Reading through the liturgies, there were moments where I simply broke into laughter, and moments where the tears began to flow freely. Above all else, I felt known as I read these prayers and owned them as my own. I felt known by God, because these prayers drew me into his presence and gave me language to bring my deepest self, warts and all, before my Father who knows me, loves me, and embraces me as I am. But I also felt known by others, who have journeyed through the same struggles and adversity, and held onto hope.

These prayers very much remind me of the Psalms, where we are invited to eavesdrop on David's brutally honest conversations with God. We very much see the agony and ecstasy: the prayers that follow victories in battle and the prayers that follow the deep grief of losing his son. We see the prayers that follow heaven's intervention and the prayers that precede any intervention, the prayers of undiluted praise and the prayers of unedited ranting, confessing and cursing. All of this is part of the human experience, and every part of the human experience is an opportunity to encounter God and be drawn into his presence.

Commenting on the Psalms, the fourth-century theologian Athanasius famously said, "most of Scripture speaks *to us*; the Psalms speak *for us*." This is why devouring the Psalms has been, throughout church history, the training ground for followers of Jesus to learn how to pray. These prayers more than just model conversations with God; they give us language to speak to God ourselves. We can find ourselves in the prayers and own them as our own.

This is why *Liturgies for Hope* is such an incredible gift to the Church. These prayers are like modern-day psalms, helping us to bring every part of our lives into conversation and communion with God. Just a brief look at the contents page will be enough to draw you in. I dare you to scan through the full list of liturgies in the contents page and then put the book down and move on. You won't be able to. There will be one liturgy that immediately captures something of your present experience, and I'm guessing curiosity as to how someone else prayed through that experience will take over. Let that curiosity do its job. You'll be led into a conversation with God that births fresh hope.

We all know that there are moments where words fail us: moments when we need to pray but can't find the words, or when words feel insufficient. The good news for those moments is that the Spirit intercedes for us (and within us) through wordless groans. There is incredible power in the groaning, wordless prayers of the saints. But there are other moments, when the words of skilled poets, whether that be David in the Psalms or Audrey and Elizabeth in this beautiful collection of prayers, are the source of great comfort, encouragement, and hope. And, after all we've been living through, the great need of our age is divine comfort, encouragement from above, and hope for what lies ahead.

So let this collection of prayers be a gift on your journey of following the way of Jesus. There will be dark valleys as well as green pastures, but you can be assured of this: with Christ as the Good Shepherd, there will always be a reason for hope.

Pete Hughes
Lead Pastor, King's Cross Church, London

Foreword by Jon Tyson

The global pandemic of 2020 hit all of us differently but profoundly. In some sense we are all still reeling from the collective trauma. Being a pastor was especially challenging, as my whole community needed tending to, and doing it in New York City— the epicenter of the crisis at the time—made it particularly challenging. Sirens sounded through the city twenty-four hours a day, carrying people in perilous condition to overwhelmed hospitals. A palpable sense of dread and fear blanketed the city.

Adding to the angst, there were so many mixed messages about what we were supposed to do, think, and believe. Both secular and religious sources got caught up in reaction and response. Fear, hysteria, misinformation, and despair were dripping the toxin of anxiety into our hearts, one update at a time. I remember grasping for what to say, some kind of comfort or lament, but words often failed me. The Psalms emerged as a source of comfort, as Scripture is timeless in a holy way, but I longed for something that would express *this* moment and carry a defiant hope, from someone who had been through it.

On Easter morning, some new liturgies began to emerge. These words seemed ancient yet immediate, and they spoke with strange authority and deep understanding. They pierced the endless noise of both local and national media and spoke to the human heart in a deep way. I kept asking where they came from and was delighted to find they were written by two women who have quietly served in our church community for some time. Audrey and Elizabeth had a front-row seat to what people in New York City were saying and feeling during those early days of the pandemic. Feeling the pain and longings of the city, they gave voice and language to what we were going through. They put pen to paper to express our collective fears, hopes, and desires and ultimately gave us words when we had none.

I hope that Audrey and Elizabeth's liturgies do the same thing for you, wherever you are and whatever you're facing. I pray that these words will draw you deeper into the love of God, help you fix your eyes on things above, and echo with the comfort of the One who is acquainted with both grief and joy.

Jon Tyson
Lead Pastor, Church of the City New York

Authors' Note

Liturgies for Hope started as an act of defiance against fear. As New York City teetered on the brink of the COVID-19 crisis in March 2020, we (Audrey and Elizabeth) asked each other, "What can we, lovers of words, create to recognize and push back the darkness?" Unsettled by the flood of frightening headlines, unhelpful think pieces, and mindless escapism, we began to wonder whether we, as writers, could create an anchor for our beloved and sorrow-stricken city to hold on to—something that would last beyond the sickness, isolation, and toilet-paper hoarding of the pandemic. So, with morning light spilling onto paper (read: keyboards) and open Bibles, we set out to put form to the shapeless depths of grief in our community.

We partnered with our church home, Church of the City New York, to publish the resulting liturgies online, launching them into the world on Easter Sunday 2020. The response was overwhelming: Our inboxes were flooded with requests to translate the liturgies into other languages, and messages from people across the world detailed exactly how the liturgies gave them hope. While *Liturgies for Hope* was born out of the specific turmoil of COVID-19, the response indicated that this collection transcends the pandemic and speaks to the evergreen needs of our time—feeling helpless, being consumed by media, worrying for physical health, needing an overdue belly laugh, and more.

Neither of us grew up in churches that practiced liturgy, yet we found that prayers rooted in the liturgical tradition proved to be a catalyst for our writing. Designed to be read and recited in community, these poetic prayers address the turmoil of the human heart and point toward the steady, unchanging truth of God's presence promised in Scripture. Liturgical prayers were written generations ago by people who observed the collapsing world around them and resolved to offer something more beautiful and trustworthy, something true, something steadying. We wanted to create a similar offering for you, whoever you are and wherever you are. These prayers are meant not to replace your prayer life but rather to awaken, encourage, and inspire it. Ultimately, each liturgy is meant to reorient your hope toward its truest Source and encourage you to press into the ache of holy longing.

We believe that God has provided truth, wisdom, and encouragement in His Word that we can recite, repeat, and meditate on—individually and corporately—and be filled and equipped for every circumstance. These liturgies were prayerfully written based on the promises of God in Scripture, and each liturgy includes a list of the verses that inspired us.

While writing these liturgies, we asked God not only "What do You want to say about this topic?" but also "What do You wish we would say to You?" We hope that these liturgies give language to the wonders and wrestling of your soul, inviting you into new depths of honesty and discovery with God. May you continue to encounter the beauty, power, and mystery of God through poetry, through prayer, and beyond.

Audrey Elledge and Elizabeth Moore
New York City

i.

Faith

STEP INTO THAT WILD, unrestrained current of hope. Allow yourself to be lifted by its waves and carried by its tide. Consider the
reasonable—or perhaps unreasonable—way that a mountain is
moved. Cling desperately to a hem. Refuse to let go until healing
comes. Be aggressively discontent with apathy, with things making
sense. Welcome questions to the table and deny fear the final
word. What is faith if not these things—ears that cannot hear but
want to, eyes that look beyond the visible to perceive the invisible?
What is faith if not remaining vulnerable enough to hope? Though
it may remain unseen, cheer for hope. Give it a standing ovation.
Clap wildly for something good that is beyond yourself. Trust that
Love will not lead you astray. Do not lose heart, but consider the
ways that you are being inwardly renewed, the ways that temporary trouble may be achieving something of greater significance.

A Liturgy for Those Who Don't Pray

For those who don't believe in God,
> may you speak tenderly to the part of yourself
> that used to hope someone was listening.

**For those who are overwhelmed with all you don't
understand,**
> may you release yourself from the burden of having all
> the answers.

For those who simply don't care,
> may you sense, deeply and innately, that you are loved.

**For those who refuse to speak to a God who
allows suffering,**
> may you find restoration and healing for the unspeak-
> able pain that you have endured.

For those who don't know how to pray but want to,
> may you begin by asking for help, as one asks a kind
> father.

Could it be that prayer is less about saying the right words
and more about the wordless cries of searching hearts?
Could it be that God is speaking not with thunderous tremors
but with gentle whispers to the soul?
Could it be that God is not angry or absent from the chaos
      of our time
but knocking on the doors of our truest selves,
waiting to be welcomed, hoping to share a meal with us?

Dear God of love,
show Yourself to us in a way that we can see.
May we sense our hearts softening within us
as You whisper to the deepest part of our souls.
May we discover true spiritual safety
and many companions to encourage us along our journey.
May cultural noise not distract or intimidate us
but guide us closer to You who understand what is beyond
      our understanding.
May we dare to imagine something greater than this tem-
      porary world
and be curious enough to uncover the riches of wisdom.
May we come to love You who love us—
You whom we do not yet see.
May we be filled with glorious and inexpressible joy by
      what we receive from You.

Prayer is not easy, nor does it make sense to many of us,
but for those who are willing to try, here is a place to begin:

"God, I want to believe, but help my unbelief.
I want to pray but don't know how.

4

Even when I don't know what to say,
You are able to interpret the groanings of my heart.
Help me, Holy Spirit.

There is so much that infuriates me about this world,
so much that I don't understand.
I don't see You in suffering.
I don't see You in injustice.
I don't even see You in Christians.
I'm asking You to show Yourself to me.
I'm open and listening.
Help me put aside what I think I know about You and get
to know the real You.
Teach me how to talk to You in a real way.

There are times when I feel I know You instinctively,
as though eternity were embedded in my own heart.
Yet there are also times when Your existence seems
preposterous.

I refuse to believe in Someone who is a figment of my
imagination.
I refuse to trust in Something that is false.
But if You are true, then even I cannot deny You.
Let the visible world reveal to me Your invisible nature.
I don't want to simply know about You, but I want to know
You.

I remain open to You,
listening for You in the deep recesses of my own heart.
Awaken me to Your nearness.

I am listening for You.

Perhaps You are listening too."

Amen.

1 Kings 19:11–13 • Job 36:26 • Psalm 34:18 • Ecclesiastes 3:11 • Isaiah 55:6–9 • Matthew 6:9–11 • Mark 9:20–24 • Luke 11:1–13 • John 3:16–17 • Romans 1:18–25; 8:26; 11:33 • 1 Corinthians 1:25 • 2 Corinthians 4:18 • 1 Peter 1:8–9 • 1 John 4:16 • Revelation 3:20

A Liturgy for Those
Wrestling with God

Here we are, Oh Lord:
creature and Creator grappling and grabbing,
all elbows and dust.
I did not expect my encounter with You to be so gritty,
so fleshy,
and did not plan to struggle in the shadows with my God.
But tonight You have come, so I trade my sleep for combat
       and my rest for sweat.

I will not let You go until You bless me.

All my longings are remembered by You,
and all my fears laid bare.
You already know what I doubt and what I seek
and the name of what I need.

Oh God of Jacob, I wrongly believed my prayer would first
        be met with an answer,
but instead, You have given me Yourself
and have met me face-to-face under the stars.
You are not a God who rebukes boldness or scorns
        audacity,
so I will stay on the mat until something moves.

I will not let You go until You bless me.

Winded and wounded, I trust that Your presence here
        means I am not forgotten.
Oh Father, You have found me in the desert and refuse to
        leave me alone,
unwilling to let Your child go down without a fight.
Only the living can wrestle,
so let me draw on Your strength,
and grant me the sort of persistence You honor.
May my outward struggle flow from the inner realization
        that
I am not grasping for straws
but rather gripping the wrists of the One who offers His
        own body,
the surest thing I can hold.

I will not let You go until You bless me.

Oh God of Israel, my bruises are proof that I was not ig-
        nored.
I have wrestled with You and triumphed,
not because I received everything I wished for

or because You succumbed to my will
but because I have been touched by the One who loves me,
crippled by grace,
and have limped into the promised land with a new name.

Amen.

Genesis 32:22–32, TLB* • Psalm 38:9 • Hosea 12:3–5

A Liturgy for Those
Deconstructing Their Faith

As you untangle the knotted history of your past
and sense the once-solid foundation shifting beneath your feet,
take courage—
for your beliefs may not be dying but awakening,
your faith may not be waning but strengthening.
You have reached the point of growth where pruning is
required,
where uprooting is needed,
where sifting through rocks and weeds is essential
to cultivating rich, fertile soil for your soul.

Do not be afraid,
for many have traveled this road before you
and have returned with a deeper understanding of what
they know
and a profound peace about what they do not.

Now is the time to be teachable,
to be circumspect without being cynical,
to learn and unlearn,
to be soft,
to listen,
to unravel the threads of what you were taught
and preserve the strands of truth—
weaving together a tapestry of wisdom.

Though it pains you to no end,
now is the time to grow out of childhood,
to crave the meatiness of truth rather than drinking what is
      easy to digest.
Now is the time to leave behind those who are always right,
who trust in their minds above anyone else's,
who leave no room for wonder and discovery.

Now is the time to have hope,
for the truth will be found by those who seek it out.
Now is the time to probe the depths of wisdom,
to explore what is gray with a sharp, clear eye,
to courageously investigate what you do not yet
      understand,
for a faith that asks questions is alive.

Questioning your faith is not a shameful thing
but rather a beautiful opportunity to have your mind
      realigned,
your heart transformed,
your soul guided home
by the One who loves you.

Many may try to discourage you,
but remember—you do not walk this valley alone.

May you find compassionate companions
who are not blinded by bitterness but open to new
        discoveries,
who are willing to wrestle with you and are anchored by
        steady hearts.
May you surround yourself with wise teachers who are
        able to guide you,
who may not have all the answers but will help you ask the
        right questions,
who are themselves lifelong students of this infinitely
        beautiful, eternally mysterious, and complex thing
        we call faith.

You are in a critical place, but take heart—
you could be on the cusp of becoming a new
        creation.
May you deconstruct in order to rebuild.
May you find steady ground and a solid rock
on which to plant your feet.
May the end of your story be deeply satisfying,
for God is leading you to the true foundation of your
        faith.
May you learn the sound of His clarifying voice
and follow your Good Shepherd when you do not know
        where to turn.
May you ask for help when you need it
and whisper the words of this simple prayer—

Oh God who does not rest until the lost sheep is found,
would You come and find me?

Amen.

Psalm 1; 23:4; 27:4; 139:6–10 • Proverbs 3:7; 11:14; 28:26 • Isaiah 41:10 • Matthew 7:7–11, 24–27; 13:3–9 • Luke 15 • John 6:63–69; 10:27–28; 15:2 • Acts 17:27 • Romans 12:2 • 2 Corinthians 5:7, 17 • Hebrews 5:13–6:3 • James 1:5 • 1 Peter 2:2–3, 25

A Liturgy for Those Who
Have Been Hurt by the Church

Oh Defender of shattered hearts,
harm has been done in Your name,
and we are among the wounded.
We bare our bruised arms before You,
battered by blows of deception,
swollen from the sting of hypocrisy.
Smitten with anger and overwhelmed with confusion,
we are disgusted by those who claim to do Your work.
You say Your church is meant to be Your beloved bride,
        Your united body,
but we have encountered divided hearts and mutilated
        limbs—
a minefield of injuries rather than a hospital for the
        sick,
individual empires rather than a sanctuary for
        Yours.

How do we live in community with those who disguise corruption as devotion?

How do we share the same faith as those who preach a gospel of love yet live lives of deceit?

How do we trust in Your goodness when those who claim Your name practice evil?

We come before You now, broken and bewildered, lamenting that Your *imago Dei* does not always bear Your image well.

May our fractured hearts not harden into bitterness but be softened by tears of grief, for You are near to every heart that has been unfairly crushed, and You are no stranger to betrayal.

How good and right it is to grieve what has brought us pain, to desire that wrongs be made right and injustice be reversed.

We leave vengeance in Your hand, where it belongs, for You do not stand idly by, ignoring wickedness, nor do You let the guilty go unpunished.

Teach us to discern between wolves in sheep's clothing and those who are truly controlled by Your Spirit.

Would You help us forgive so that we may begin to heal?

Would You soften our hearts and remind us of the beauty that is possible in Your church?

For we are recipients of Your undeserved forgiveness and beneficiaries of Your infinite mercy.

Let us never think, Oh Lord, that we are better than the
one who has hurt us,
for we once owed You an immeasurable debt that was canceled on the cross.

Restore Your church, Oh God, and do not abandon us.
Have mercy on us, Your people, and lead us out of our
idolatrous ways.
Would Your kindness bring us to repentance so that these
wounds may be healed?
Would You transform us from the inside out until we are
true reflections of You?
There has been so much devastation at the hands of Your
people,
and we lift our cry of sorrow to You, Oh Healer and
Redeemer.

How we ache for the marriage supper of the Lamb,
when Your bride will be purged of corruption and
adorned with righteousness,
when the purity of Your ways will be written on her heart,
when she will know You to her core and be so utterly
healed that she harms no longer.

Amen.

Exodus 34:7 • Psalm 34:18 • Isaiah 63:7–17 • Jeremiah 31:31–34 • Matthew 7:15–20;
18:21–35; 23:13–39 • Mark 2:17 • Luke 22 • Romans 2:4; 12:2, 19 • Ephesians 2:1–9;
5:25–27 • Colossians 2:13–14 • Revelation 19:6–10

A Liturgy for Those Embracing the Mystery of Faith

When we question everything we once thought we
       believed,
help us, Gentle Teacher, to be brave explorers of the
       unknown.
When doubts multiply in our minds,
help us not to be afraid but to be curious.
When questions arise about Your existence,
    Your goodness,
      the way of Your salvation,
help us press in and believe that You are present in the
       mystery.

Teacher, we're longing for someone to give us assurance.
We measure You with our own intellect,
looking for answers from books, academia, pop culture,
       and critics.

But faith is impossible when we seek it within the bounds
of our understanding.
We become fools when we claim to be wise.
So help us reach beyond what we know.
Help us step into wonder,
into learning,
into trusting You for flourishing.
The adventure of faith is there.

We are like sheep without a shepherd,
listening to the wisdom of the world,
allowing ourselves to be discipled by culture.
Would You liberate us from our compulsive need to
understand?
Would You marvelously kindle our imaginations?
Would You help us hold space for not knowing?
For being wrong?
For trusting You with what we can't comprehend?
Give us a spirit of humility all the days of our lives so we
keep coming back to You.

Oh God, echoes of Your essence vault across the sky from
sunrise to sunset.
Help us seek You with urgency and wonder,
with childlikeness instead of childishness,
until a foundation of faith—sturdy and timeless—is
revealed.
Warm our hearts to faith and wonder as we wait for You.
Though we bring more questions than answers,
though the discomfort of doubt threatens to unravel us,
in faith we treasure the tension of this promise:

With man, this is impossible.
With God, all things are possible.

Keep us alive in our famine of faith until we become what
we believe.
In weakness, yes, we do believe.
Help our unbelief.

Amen.

Psalm 19; 27:13–14; 139:1–6, 17–18 • Isaiah 53:6 • Jeremiah 17:7–9 • Matthew 7:7–8;
9:27–30; 18:2–4; 19:26 • Mark 9:23–25 • Romans 1:21–23 • Ephesians 5:12–14 • Hebrews 11:1–3

A Liturgy for Those Who Worship the Wrong Thing

Oh Lord, we were knit in the womb to worship,
but how quickly our adoration splits and refracts when we
        cannot touch Your face.
Impatient, we trade our inheritance for pocket change,
our banquet for scraps,
our life for death.

We have neither melted gold nor carved from stone,
but we have fashioned idols with our own hands,
master craftsmen who are
craving, thirsting, seeking
what is not You.

We can list our golden calves by name:
sex,

money,

power,

comfort,

approval.

But, Oh Father, unclench our tight fists so we can see the
false gods we have made of Your blessings:

family,

health,

cities,

vocation,

coffee.

We confess the disordered loves we have never examined.

Oh Lord, we settle for so little.

You are a jealous God,

and Your perfect love will not stand to see us on bended
knees before any throne but Your own.

Help us to trust the nail-haunted hands that loosen our
grip

on what we have placed before You.

Oh Christ, may we lose our appetite for artificial joy,

instead hungering for what is real.

May we tire of serving multiple masters

and ache for the affections of One.

May we set the cross at the center of our gaze.

May we proclaim, with reordered hearts,

that only You can satisfy,

that only in You is our hope secure.

May the emptiness of our own creations
point us to the fullness of You.

Amen.

Exodus 20:3–6; 32:1–6; 34:14 • Psalm 16:4; 115; 139:13 • Jeremiah 10:3–16 • Habakkuk 2:18 • Matthew 6:24 • Acts 17:29 • Romans 1:25 • Colossians 3:5–6 • 1 Thessalonians 1:9–10 • Hebrews 6:19

A Liturgy for Those Struggling
with Secret Sin

Oh God who sees in the dark,
we are lonely.

We crave comfort, pleasure, and connection
to fill the sense that something is missing.
We long to be seen, delighted in, wanted, and loved
to confirm that we are enough.

Our brains and bodies grasp for immediate gratification
when what we really need is You.
Oh Fountain of living water,
well up in our hearts until we are overflowing with everlasting life.

When we are broken, You make us whole.
When we are consumed with desire, You fill the gap.

When we stumble again and again and again, You forgive.
When our flesh fails, You strengthen our hearts.
God, we want to choose You forever.

But our flesh is weak and will lead us to death if we let it—
and we have let it.
We have accumulated heavy weights of guilt.
We have fled to the shadows of isolation and shame.
We have relied on our own willpower to free us from this
        prison of flesh.

Oh Jesus, You know what it is to be human and tempted.
Teach us how to die to our flesh and ask Your Spirit for
        help.
Lead us to Your heart of grace and compassion.
Lead us out of darkness and into the blinding freedom of
        Light.
Lead us out of hiding and into beautiful communities of
        confession,
even if we are confessing the same thing over and over for
        a while.

May we fill our minds with true and noble things.
May we sit in beautiful spaces, consuming Your loveliness.
May we consider what is excellent and praiseworthy.
May we practice thanksgiving and receive Your peace.
May we contemplate Your kindness and be led to
        repentance.

Oh Healer and Redeemer, reach into the darkest corners
        of our hearts,

and shine Your light there.

We cry out to You in the midst of our sin and fall on Your
mercy.

We come into Your presence for healing, longing to hear
these words:

Neither do I condemn you; go and sin no more.

We are powerless to free ourselves from sin.

So set us free, Holy Spirit. Set us free.

Amen.

Psalm 25:11; 73:25–26; 86:5; 139:11–12 • Isaiah 9:2 • Matthew 26:41 • Luke 4:1–13;
9:23–24 • John 4:7–15; 8:10–12, NKJV;* 16:7–13 • Romans 2:4; 6:23; 8:1–2, 5–6 • Acts
13:38–39 • 1 Corinthians 9:25–27; 10:13 • 2 Corinthians 3:17; 4:5–6 • Galatians 5:16–
24 • Ephesians 2:1–8 • Philippians 4:8 • James 5:16 • 1 Peter 2:9–11 • 1 John 1:9

A Liturgy for Those Who
Have Been Complicit in Injustice

Oh Merciful God,
in fear we have sheltered ourselves from the injustice of the
       world;
we have turned away from suffering instead of bearing
       witness to it;
we have withheld our time, our compassion, and our
       resources,
prioritizing convenience instead of joining You in the work
       of renewing all things.

Lord, Your loving arms embrace the vulnerable;
Your tender hands caress the brokenhearted;
Your crystal-clear voice declares that the captives are set free.
And You have invited us to be ambassadors of Your gospel
       in this new era of grace,
to announce Your comfort to all who are steeped in sorrow,

to offer Your strength to all who are crushed by despair,
to wrap Your cloak of joy around the shoulders of all who
    weep.

Yet we confess that we have not laid down our lives for the
    sake of those who need You most.
We have not gone out of our way to love.
We have not fed the hungry, tended the sick, or clothed the
    naked.
Whether from ill intent or apathy, we have allowed
    wickedness to continue
and dishonored You by dismissing the needs of Your beloved.

In full view of our faithlessness
and with hearts that long to know the fear of the
    Lord—we repent.
We set our hearts to seek You again,
for You are the defender and upholder of truth.

Where we have sowed indifference,
may we sow obedience.
Where we have sowed fear,
may we sow openness and love.
Where we have trusted in our own way,
may we turn and seek Your way, Oh Lord.
Break up our fallow ground,
and arouse in us a desire for uprightness.
Make us restless for as long as injustice prevails.

We acknowledge that activism is incomplete and short-
    lived without You,

so infuse our justice work with Your tenderness and victory.
Help us remain connected to You, our true vine and source
       of life,
so that the bringing of justice is also the bringing of love.

Awaken us if we are sleepwalking through the motions,
and silence the fruitless noise of clanging gongs and clash-
       ing cymbals.
May the pure notes of Your freedom resound all the more
as we are continually drawn into Your orbit of love.

We bless You, Oh Lord, for there is no injustice with You.
May we partner with You in rebuilding the ruins of the
       past,
for You are the architect of new life.
May former devastations be brought to their full end
and patterns of pain be disrupted and healed.
May the bodies that were broken be renewed
and the riches that were lost be restored.

May the peace of Christ rule in our hearts
as we seek to be a unified body—
a mosaic of broken individuals
made whole by the blood of Jesus.

Amen.

Leviticus 19:9–18 • 1 Chronicles 19:1–9 • 2 Chronicles 7:14 • Psalm 34:18 • Proverbs
22:8–9; 28:13 • Isaiah 43:18–19; 61 • Hosea 10:12–13 • Joel 2:13 • Matthew 25:35–40
• Mark 12:28–34 • Luke 4:14–21 • John 15:5–13 • Acts 3:19 • Romans 2:4; 9:14–18 •
1 Corinthians 13 • 2 Corinthians 5:11–21 • Colossians 3:15 • 2 Peter 3:9 • 1 John 1:9

ii.

Vocation

THOUGH OUR SPIRITS ROAM outside time and space, our bodies remain grounded in the here and now, in the mercies of the earth, in the tactile and the finite. Though we cannot number our days, we know that they are numbered. For a brief time, we put our natural talents, our learned skills, our unique abilities to use for the flourishing of others, exploring what it is to be made, to imitate a Maker, to be trusted with creating, innovating, producing, and restoring. Even the work of our hands is sacred, done by us but not for us, as we rejoice in our createdness, in our stewardship of a kingdom unfolding. As we strive toward an end we cannot wholly fathom, may we recognize the honor of handling, forming, and ascribing meaning to life. May we enjoy our part in bringing order to the world. May we discover the eternal purpose that guides our tasks, the power by which we live and move and have our being. May we labor for love and not for recognition, celebrating the simple work, the unadorned acts, the hidden endeavors that go without accolade. May we hold the specificity of our profession loosely, remaining open to the way our tasks change with the seasons. May we do all of this in the presence of love. For the work we do is not for ourselves, nor even solely for others, but for the One who made us.

A Liturgy for Those Who Don't Love Their Job

How long, Oh Lord,
must I be reminded of the disconnect between my soul
     and the work of my hands?
Everywhere I turn, the repetitive chants of
calling
and *passion*
and *vocation*
strike a blow to my weary heart,
for I have not yet found these things, though I have
     searched for them like treasure.

Since those sinless days in the garden, You have called
     work *very good,*
but I have not known the particular taste of this
     blessing.

I feel so distant from the paradise in which work was
      wrought
and so envious of those who wake up without the dread
      and indifference I have come to wear
as easily as skin.
Guard my hope, Oh God, against the cynicism that is
      determined to weaken it.

In You, there is nothing I truly lack.
All salvation, purpose, worth, and peace were sealed at
      Calvary,
yet I still long to see these things reflected in my work,
to feel as if my resurrected self is contributing to the
      expansion of Your kingdom in a meaningful way.
Just as You created beauty and order from the formless void,
so I desire to have a job where I can do the same.

Oh Teacher, help me to have a right view of work.
Rid me of the idea that there is a single job designed for
      me—
a soulmate sort of calling—
and do not let me spend my whole life in search of it.
Guide me so I do not mistake normal frustration and the
      daily grinding of routine
for evidence of a wrong career.
Instead, confirm if there is a true mismatch between my
      gifts and my work,
and reveal where the needs of this world are not met by
      my placement in this job
or where I am serving a vision that does not align with
      Yours.

Some days I cannot even name what I am after,
so relieve me with the knowledge that my yearnings are
already known by You.
Receive me with grace as I boldly approach Your throne,
asking for an open door.
If it is in Your will, Oh Perfect Father, bring a job made for
me with such precision,
such care and intimate detail,
that I cannot help but claim it wholeheartedly, as a child
receives a gift tailor-made for them.
Do not let me be swayed by the hope of wealth or prestige
or even of ease
but rather by the givenness of this work from You.

As I wait for the fulfillment of this longing,
I will turn my eyes back to this job I do not love
and arrive with my full self, working as if working unto You.
At the close of each day, may I feel without hesitation that
I have served You well,
and may You call the work of my hands *very good*.
May the people I work with notice a joyous gusto
and a renewed tenderness of spirit.
Oh Lord, it will take faith to leave this job, and it will take
faith to stay,
so help me choose, with wisdom and clarity, that which is
the most loving.

Amen.

Genesis 2:15 • Psalm 13:1–2; 34:10; 90:17 • Proverbs 14:30 • Matthew 6:26 • 1 Corinthians 15:58 • Colossians 3:17, 23–24 • Hebrews 4:16; 6:10

A Liturgy for Paying Bills When There's Not Enough Money

Jehovah Jireh,
we are struggling to trust that You will provide.
As we spend every paycheck on necessities for ourselves
      and our families,
we are constantly aware of how much we lack.
As we look at what we have versus what we owe,
we don't see how there will ever be enough.
Our instinct is to double down on worry,
to take matters into our own hands and be greedy with
      every dollar.

Even now, Oh Lord, let us look for ways to be generous.
Let us expect You to provide.
Let us be good stewards of the little we have
so that we may be trusted with sacred riches.

You are the God who nourished the Israelites in the
       wilderness,
who turned water into wine,
who fed five thousand with a handful of loaves and fish.
We tell ourselves these stories of Your kindness
to remember that You are an abundant provider.
You may not always give in the way that we ask,
but You will always provide exactly what we need,
for even when we are faithless, You remain faithful.

So when our minds begin to spiral into worry
and when it looks like our ends will not meet,
may we cling to Your promise that there will always be
       enough.
Our oil will not run out.
Our wells will not run dry.
We boldly ask You for provision, Lord,
and we hold You to Your promises.

May we entrust our lives, our bills, and our bank accounts
       to You.
May we commit our salaries, our investments, and our
       assets to Your care.
All of it is Yours, Lord, given to us to steward temporarily.
We do not worship our wealth,
nor do we despair at poverty.
Rather, we draw near to You.

We look to the sparrows for guidance.
We consider the lilies for advice.

They do not needlessly toil or worry beyond what they can
      see.
We lift up our eyes to soaring hills—
from where does our help come?
Our help comes from our Father,
who lavishes us with the unsearchable riches of Christ.

Give us the faith, Oh God, to trust You for what we do not
      have.
Give us cheerful hearts of generosity, even if our contribu-
      tions seem meager.
Give us riches that do not run out and hearts that rejoice
      over treasure in heaven.
Give us lightened loads so we may carry on with simple,
      joy-filled lives.

Hear us as we cry,
Make us like the sparrows, God! Dress us like the lilies!
Our hearts are stilled by Your reply:
Oh My children, how much more you are to Me than they.

Amen.

1 Kings 17:8–16 • Psalm 105:40–45; 121 • Matthew 6:19–20; 14:13–21; 25:14–30 •
Luke 12:22–34 • John 2:1–11 • 2 Corinthians 9:7–8 • Ephesians 3:8 • Philippians 4:11–
13, 19 • 2 Timothy 2:13 • Hebrews 13:5 • 1 Peter 4:19

A Liturgy for Gardening

Lord of the sun and soil and everything in between,
bless our gardening hands with the softness of patience,
with an unhurried cadence,
and with the surety that more will grow than was sown.

Giver of life, bless these seeds,
which will produce a surplus of fruit despite their size,
and remind us of the sufficiency of seed-sized faith.

Sustaining God, bless this dirt,
which must first be broken before it yields,
and show us how the shattered places within us are fertile
    ground too.

Loving Creator, bless this water as it falls like rain,
soaking the earth like the word that goes from Your mouth,
never returning empty or void.

Perfect Vine, bless this pruning,
this cleansing that prepares us for the hope of harvest.

Gentle Teacher, bless these blooms and fruit
as they call us to consider how to live without toil,
and remind us that growth takes time
but will surely come when we are rooted and abiding in
        You.

And, Lord of all, bless these plants to grow
as living remembrances of the garden we lost
and of the paradise we will soon regain.

Amen.

Isaiah 55:10–15 • Matthew 17:20 • Luke 8:4–15; 12:27; 17:6 • John 15:1–17 • 2 Corinthians 9:6 • Colossians 2:6–7

A Liturgy for Learning a New Skill

How wonderful, Oh God, is the gift of curiosity.
The first task You gave humankind was to study the world,
and even now, we still delight in uncovering what You have
      concealed.

There is a surplus of things I do not yet know:
hobbies and languages,
skills and subjects.
As I set my heart on learning this new thing,
keep me childlike in my approach:
    inquisitive and open,
    determined and delighted.
As a child does not berate herself for falling while starting
      to walk,
so shall I unashamedly persist in my learning,
certain that You will lead me as I go.

Jesus, when You walked this earth, You often answered
      questions with questions,
asking us to consider more deeply before making
      conclusions.
In this new pursuit, teach me how to also ask the right
      things.
Show me how to probe beneath the surface of what I can
      see
and how to persevere when the romance of curiosity
      wanes
and the discipline of commitment must be practiced.
Oh Christ, when I reach the limits of my human mind,
help me to embrace mystery over mastery.

There is a whole world I will not discover this side of
      eternity,
yet I thank You, Lord, for giving me even the smallest
      glimpse before the final curtain falls.
May I not fall prey to tunnel vision or selfishness
but instead consider how I am better equipped to serve
      and love with the new things I know.
May I be eager to share what I learn in this process,
not hoarding knowledge as if it is scarce or parading it like
      a trophy that can be won
but sharing generously the treasures I have dug.

Amen.

Genesis 2:19–20 • Psalm 92:5; 111:2 • Proverbs 25:2 • Matthew 18:4 • 1 Corinthians
8:1 • Philippians 1:6

A Liturgy for Those Working
Through the Night

Oh Lord, I am tired,
so please be near.
Many are the things that must get done,
and little is the time I have.
I possess few words to ask for what I need, so, Holy Spirit,
intercede with groans to express what I cannot.

Jesus, be the mediator between me and this never-ending
       work.
Multiply the waning hours from now until dawn like You
       did with those loaves and fish.

Prince of Peace, rule in my heart as I finish what must get
       done,
and forgive this weak flesh that curls up in the garden in-
       stead of waiting on You.

Merciful Father who does not slumber,
lift my heavy eyes and remind me where my help comes
       from.

Perfect Provider, grant me perseverance to finish what feels
       impossible without You.

Even if I do not feel as if I am changing the world,
teach me how to steward this hidden work with joy instead
       of grumbling.
May I do this night work heartily and gratefully—
with my fullest and truest self—
as to You and not to others.

Oh Lord, I am tired,
so please be near.

Amen.

Psalm 34:17–18; 121; 130:6 • Matthew 14:13–21; 26:36–45 • Romans 8:26–27 • Philippians 2:14; 4:13 • Colossians 3:15, 23 • 1 Timothy 2:5

A Liturgy for Those Who Are Too Busy

Oh Lord, when I cannot seem to slow the pace of my life,
when each day seems to outrun me and every moment
      bleeds into the next,
would You give me the wisdom to know what to keep and
      what to let go?

I am tempted to double down on control,
to salvage every shred of time,
losing myself in a tangled web of frenetic anxiety,
struggling to differentiate between what is essential and
      what is not.
Like Martha, I am exasperated and troubled by many
      things,
desperate for You to see my hustling,
longing for You to affirm my contributions.

Even now, may I withdraw to the secret place,
to that sacred sanctuary where my inner being meets Yours.
Would You whisper to my heart Your gentle reminder:
that only one thing is necessary—
to sit at Your feet,
to listen to Your voice,
to absorb revelations from You.
May I choose this good portion,
this freedom from striving,
this being still and knowing that You are God;
for the way of surrender produces a steady peace that can
        never be lost.

May I not be afraid to pause and rest,
trusting that what needs to get done will get done.
May I enjoy the freedom of being undistracted
and listen to Your reassuring voice.
May I breathe deeply of Your love and be refreshed
as I take on the posture of a child,
of an unhurried daughter or son.
May I learn from Your gentle and lowly heart,
and may my burdens be lightened as I delight in Your way.

Here is my time, Lord.
I offer it to You, not as a display of my worth
but as an outpouring of love.

Amen.

Psalm 46:10 • Matthew 11:25–30 • Luke 10:38–42

A Liturgy for Creativity

Oh Creator of the ends of the earth,
the heavens are shouting Your significance;
the skies are singing of Your wondrous mystery.
If day to day pours forth speech, let me listen.
If night after night displays knowledge, let me be a student
      of the stars.

We are created to create, no matter who we are.
We are not artists or scientists, teachers or tradesmen—
we are the *imago Dei.*
Let us walk in the good works You've created for us.

May we build into our day rhythms of rest.
May our lives ebb and flow with reflection and expression.
May we surround ourselves with empty spaces for listening.

May our crafts be poems of praise to You, wholly original
and breathtaking.

We do not create, Oh God, to bring glory to
ourselves;
rather, when we create, we are overshadowed by the
wonder of Your glory.
Let us never worship our art, but let us be enraptured by
You.
May whatever we create echo Your nature and radiate
Your goodness.

Together we enter into this secret, sacred space.
Together we are eager for the brand-new thing that is
about to emerge.
Together we acknowledge that this process of creation is
holy.

Optional Ending for Writers

May we trust You with the words that come,
not prematurely judging them as insufficient but believing
they have purpose and beauty.
May our language be clear and concise, brimming with the
wisdom of simplicity.
May our ideas be thoughtful and productive, promoting
both critical thinking and unity.
May the spirit behind our words be of truth and of love so
that they withstand the test of time and perhaps
bring life for generations to come.

Accept these words as a sacrifice of praise to You.

Keep our hearts wholly devoted to You.

Amen.

Genesis 1:27 • Psalm 19:1–2; 108:1–5; 115:1 • Isaiah 64:8 • Romans 1:19–20 • Ephesians 2:10; 4:15

A Liturgy for Caregivers

Oh Healer and Restorer of life, we are weary.
You have called us into work that, at times, feels like more
        than we can bear.
We have sat at bedsides and breakfast tables, in hospital
        rooms and clinics,
witnessing the persistent cycle of sickness and healing,
only to come home exhausted and discouraged.

God of Jacob, cast Your gaze upon us.
You promised that when we pass through the waters, You
        will be with us;
and though the rivers rage, they will not overwhelm us;
and though we walk through fire, we will not be burned.

But we have only so much energy,
only so much compassion,

only so much endurance,
to carry on in our own strength.

Therefore, God of all comfort, turn and be gracious to us,
 for we cry to You and only You.
Refuge and Strength, renew our trust in You until we
 mount up with wings of eagles.
When we are empty, would You lead us to Your wellspring
 of living water?
When we are hopeless, would You lift up our eyes to see
 the unseen?
When we are lonely, would You give us life-giving communities to remind us that we are not enduring alone?

Would You heal the sick, both physically and spiritually, as
 they cope with their unique and painful maladies?
Would You give us the words to comfort those who are
 grieving?
Would You give us wisdom to discern the best treatments
 and ways to serve?
Would You grant us perseverance even as we are burning
 out and daily bearing the suffering of others?

Even now, we wait for You more than watchmen wait for
 morning.
Even now, we learn the way of gentleness through Your
 humble heart.
Even now, we hope in a better future, believing You are
 making all things new.
Even now, we are oaks of righteousness, a planting of the
 Lord for the display of Your splendor.

Oh God who holds our times in Your hand,
we ask that You hasten pain and suffering to a swift end.
May a period of rest, peace, and bounty follow
when the days of mourning have ceased and life is
       restored.

Amen.

Psalm 23; 25:16–21; 27; 31:15; 46; 91; 130:6 • Isaiah 40:31; 43:1–2; 53:3; 61:1–4 •
Habakkuk 3:17–19 • Matthew 11:28–30 • John 4:10 • Romans 5:3–5 • 2 Corinthians
1:3–5 • James 1:5 • Jude 24 • Revelation 21:3–5

iii.

Health

BREATHE IN AND REMEMBER you are dust. Breathe out and know you are eternal. Revel in the mystery that you—in this body and with this mind—can be both at once. Befriend the arduous and fleeting pull of gravity on your flesh. If everything is here today and gone tomorrow, then so, too, is this body: a temple made of breath. Do not take for granted the mornings you wake with fizz in your bones and life in your eyes. Use it to draw close to others. And then do not take for granted the mornings you wake with pain beneath your skin and clouds in your mind. Use it to draw close to others. There will be days when you lower the mat, and days when you are on the mat being lowered. Count it all as grace. In times of strength, tithe your energy, giving it away in service of others. In times of weakness, discover the medicinal power of pausing. Trust that rest can be an extravagant protest against a world that treats you like a machine. Trade production for softness, and see how your value never wavers. Give thanks for your particular parts, even when they hurt. Your lungs, your nose, your heart—all handmade for you, like gifts you never asked for. Be afflicted by hope as you inch—or hurtle—toward resurrection.

A Liturgy for Those Worried
for Their Physical Health

Every ache and pain,
sniffle and cough,
fever and shallow breath,
is a threat
enlarging in our minds until we are consumed with anxiety
       for the health of our bodies.
Our interior selves become children afraid of the dark,
       covers pulled up to our noses,
eyes darting from shadow to shadow, flinching at every
       sound,
until we are certain there is a monster in the closet or an
       intruder on the stairs.

Oh God, may our minds not run away with what-ifs or
       irrational fears.
Help us breathe, wait, and listen to the bodies You formed

from the dust of the ground and the breath of
Your nostrils.
Help us observe our symptoms (or lack thereof) correctly.
Help us discipline our minds, not to despair at worst-case
scenarios but instead to accurately interpret our
current moment, seeking Your wisdom for the next
rational step.

May we trust You with our bodies, which creak and groan
with mortality.
May our physical fragility remind us of our dependence on
You.
May we rejoice in our weakness, knowing that You are strong.
May we develop a robust courage that does not fear our
weakening bodies.
May we look forward to the day when we will receive ever-
lasting bodies and be reunited with You.

God, You are the One who forgives our sins and heals us
of disease.
We ask for physical healing when we need it,
for a correct perspective of the brevity of sickness in light
of eternity,
for deep joy to well up in our souls because we know we
are secure,
for hearts that look forward to boundless shalom.

Amen.

Genesis 2:7 • Psalm 94:19; 103:1–3 • Romans 8:18–30 • 1 Corinthians 15:35–58 • 2
Corinthians 12:9–10 • 2 Timothy 1:7 • James 1:5

A Liturgy for Those Prone to Binging

Oh child of God, take heart, for He does not hold your
     binging against you.

You live in a world with so much to devour: food, shows,
     media, sleep.
When you feel as if your flesh has won again, indulging to
     the point of sickness,
you are still freer than you realize and more loved than you know.

Examine what lies at the root of your binge:
pain, fear, sadness, boredom.
Not one of these feelings is unseen by God.
He does not condemn you when you go numb
but rather calls you into the glorious and delicious
     discipline of feasting on Him instead.

But even when you are more full on creation than
　　　Creator,
you are still freer than you realize and more loved than you
　　　know.

Perhaps your tendency toward excess is a belief that God
　　　will not provide.
Like the Israelites who did not trust that they would receive
　　　fresh manna each day,
you have learned to create your own stores and guard
　　　yourself with gluttony.
But even when you feel as if you cannot break free of these
　　　self-protective instincts
and question if tomorrow will really work out for your
　　　good,
you are still freer than you realize and more loved than you
　　　know.

Do not resign yourself to a life in which your flesh is always
　　　at war with your soul—
it will not feel this hard forever.
You are still a new creation.
Remember that self-control is not a reward for the
　　　disciplined but rather a beautiful outcome of living
　　　in step with the Spirit.
God's mercies are new each morning, so leave behind
　　　what belongs in the shadows and stay in the
　　　light.
You are freer than you realize and more loved than you
　　　know.

Oh child of God, take heart, for He does not hold your
binging against you.

Amen.

Exodus 16 • Proverbs 25:16 • Lamentations 3:22–23 • Romans 8:1–4, 28; 12:1; 13:14
• 1 Corinthians 6:19–20; 10:31 • 2 Corinthians 5:17 • Galatians 5:1, 22–23 • 2 Timothy
1:7 • 1 Peter 2:11

A Liturgy for Fasting

Forgive me, Father, for I have delighted in Your blessings
       more than I have delighted in You.
Like a child creating sandcastles, I have built routines and
       habits around Your gifts,
unaware of their fragility and dependent on them for joy.
Lately I have padded myself with creature comforts that
       bury my eternal longings until they are scarcely
       felt, hardly pulsing.
So here I am, abstaining from the good in pursuit of the
       Better.

Oh Jesus, I long to grieve Your absence,
to rightly feel the sting of dependence on You,
to let You take first place in all things.
Today I fast when my flesh roars *feast,*

because earthly abundance has hidden Your face from view.
Show me how You did this for forty days—
   how the Word became food
   and prayer became life.
Remind me how You are often found where scarcity is felt.

In this fast, may the space between heaven and earth grow
      thin.
As I empty myself, may the acoustics of my heart
      transform so I can hear Your voice,
the gentlest of whispers often muffled when I'm full.

You do not demand that I fast
but rather invite me into this voluntary surrender for my
      good.
Today I inhale mercy and exhale grace,
trusting that You are the only one who nourishes and
      sustains.

Oh Lord, You say that some things change only through
      prayer and fasting.
I'm so eager for You to move,
so here I stand at Your door: asking, seeking, pounding.
But if nothing breaks
or alters
or shifts monumentally from this fast
yet I still learn to better recognize Your voice,
to grow fonder of my Creator,
to root myself deeper in love,
then, Oh Father, it was worth it.

Invite me into holy restraint, Oh God.

Put a seal over my mouth so that I do not brag about my
    sacrifice

or expect applause for my grit

but rather relish the beauty of sharing a secret discipline
    with You.

Oh my soul, do not strain for a reward.

Live quietly, and ask for a multiplication of strength

so that you can fast for both yourself and others.

Remember that weakness comes before breakthrough.

Amen.

Psalm 141:3 • Isaiah 58:6 • Matthew 6:16–18; 7:7–8; 9:15; 17:21 • Luke 4:1–13 • John
6:35 • 2 Corinthians 12:9

A Liturgy for a Lunch Break

Oh Bread of Life, join me in this midday sabbath
as I pause my labors to nourish my body and rest from all
        striving.
Be so near that it is as if You have pulled up a seat next to
        me,
my greatest confidant and friend.

Even if I am constrained by time,
unbind me from the haste that fills my spirit,
and teach me the way of unhurriedness.
May I be conscious of each bite,
properly enjoying the blessing of this lunch and
ever mindful of the way even chewing can be a prayer.

Bless this food as it meets my taste buds,
delighting me with new flavors and pleasing textures.

Bless this meal as it enters my body,
fortifying me with energy for the remainder of the day.
Bless my stomach as it is filled,
and so, too, fill my spirit, which hungers for a word from
        You.

May this meal refuel what has been depleted
and resurrect what was eroded by the grind of the day.
As I eat, restore the fruit of Your Spirit in me, Oh God.
With this bite, may I increase in love.
With the next, may I overflow with joy.
May I breathe in peace.
May I strengthen in patience.
May I grow in kindness.
May I radiate goodness.
May I remember faithfulness.
May I dress myself in gentleness.
May I embody self-control.

Most of all, may I return to my work softer in presence
        and stronger in spirit,
more loving in my actions and generous in my thoughts,
because of this lunch break with You.

Amen.

Matthew 11:28–30 • John 6:35; 15:15 • Galatians 5:22–23

A Liturgy for Going on a Walk

Oh Lord, I praise You for this body You have knit to hold
      me together,
to carry my heart and mind across plains and pavement.
I confess that walking has become so commonplace that
I do not often consider the mechanics of this frame that
      pulls me through life
or the specificity of Your design.
So today as I walk,
keep me ever mindful of the glorious gift it is to move un-
      fettered through creation
beside the One who made me.

Oh God, awaken my senses so I can notice what I once
      took for granted:
the breeze on my face,
the tenor of a neighbor's voice,

the smell of a meal wafting through windows,
the therapy of birdsong.
Help me trade efficiency for attention, carelessness for
        consideration.
Show me how Your power and gentleness are woven into
        this world
and how not even a crack in the sidewalk has arisen
        without Your say.
May my walk turn to worship as I remember that
from You and through You and for You are all things,
including this street that I tread.

Oh Father, if I should pass anyone as I walk this road,
may they encounter a spirit so buoyant,
a peace so consuming,
a light so lovely,
that they cannot help but turn their eyes upward in search
        of the Source.
Let me not forget that if my body is a temple
and the home in which Your Son—the hope of glory—
        chooses to dwell,
then every step I take becomes holy ground,
ripe with divine possibility.

In walking,
I am reminded that I tread a world that will spin on its axis
        without my help,
that will breathe and grow and live without effort or input
        on my part.
I am reminded that I am made of dust and bound by time
as I travel this earth,

and I cannot arrive any quicker than human feet can carry
me.
To walk is to embrace the mystery of Emmanuel,
of God with us,
who once slowed His own pace and gathered dirt on His
soles.
This is what life following Christ is like:
not a sprint,
not an uphill climb,
not a trudging crawl,
but a walk—putting one foot in front of the other, moving
by faith and not sight,
keeping in step with You.

Amen.

Psalm 139:13–14 • Matthew 1:23; 6:26–30 • Romans 11:36 • 1 Corinthians 6:19 • 2
Corinthians 5:7 • Colossians 1:27 • 1 John 1:7

A Liturgy for Falling Asleep

Meet me, Oh Lord, as I close my eyes,
ready to exchange toil for rest,
noise for quiet,
exhaustion for restoration.

The troubles of my heart have multiplied,
but I lay each one at the feet of the One who never
      slumbers.
Oh God of refuge, You are greater than my buzzing thoughts
and caffeinated veins
and unchecked lists
and regrets from a day in which I feel I did nothing great
      for You.
I do not earn my sleep but rather receive it like a child
from You, Abba, who call me beloved.

The predictability of sleep falters now,
but I rest in the One who is the same yesterday, tonight,
      and forever.
Remind me, Oh Christ, that You will finish what I have left
      undone.
I lie under the starry hosts that You call by name
and trust that when I awake, I will still be with
      You.

Oh Great Shepherd, thank You for leading this worn
      body
beside quiet waters,
for inviting me to cease striving.

Tonight lead me in the way everlasting
so when I awake, I can love my neighbors
and serve Your world
with readiness
and vigor
and rested love.

Amen.

Optional Breathing Exercise

Lord, I inhale Your presence
and exhale my fear.
I inhale Your promises
and exhale my dread.
I inhale Your safety

and exhale my racing mind.
I inhale You
and exhale me.

Psalm 4:8; 23:1–3; 25:17; 121; 127:2; 139:18, 24 • Isaiah 40:26 • Matthew 11:28–30 •
Romans 8:15 • Hebrews 13:8

A Liturgy for Those Who
Wake in the Night

Oh Father of stillness,
You reside in the quiet corners of the night.
The world may be sleeping,
but You are keeping watch.

When I wake, You are here.
When I toss and turn, You are here.
When my mind races, You are here.
When I fear the dark, You are here.

Your loving gaze does not waver in the shadows,
and You are not threatened by this absence of light.
Your peaceful presence cannot be kidnapped by darkness,
for You are the creator of night:

    the father of stars,

the designer of depths,
the master of mysteries.

Whether I lie awake for moments or hours,
may my heart incline toward You.
May I not be anxious as I await sleep
but enjoy these hushed moments of wakefulness with You.

May I hand You,
one at a time,
the matters that are troubling my spirit:
  the unfinished work,
  the unresolved conflicts,
  the unsettling worries,
  the unstable relationships.
Would You take them, Lord?
Would You help me release these cares into Your capable
      hands?

I am listening.
I am here with You.
I am awake and unafraid.
Is there anything You would like to tell me?

Amen.

Psalm 121; 139

A Liturgy for Those Deprived of Touch

I will not sugarcoat this, Oh Lord:
I long to be touched by someone who loves me.
There is no quick fix for this poverty of touch,
as I have determined not to settle for cheap affection
and will not stir up love before it is ready.
But it would be dishonest to say that my body does not
        ache for an embrace
or that my skin does not feel mired in loneliness.
Oh Maker, please be close.

How beautiful that You understand the constraints of
        human flesh,
that You know what I feel when I am alone.
Oh High Priest who sympathizes with my weaknesses,
I do not want to feel embarrassed by talking with You
        about this need,

for You are the God who came to earth and touched
        others with care.

Oh Christ, You set an example of loving humanity with
        Your hands:
the blind man whose eyes You touched with spit and
        mud,
the disciples whose feet You washed,
the children You held,
the woman You blessed when she grabbed Your
        hem.
Touch is essential in the kingdom of God.

Remind me of the healing already at my disposal:
my ability to hug and to hold.

Grant me discernment so I can touch with honor.
May I always aim to serve rather than take,
rejoicing in shared humanity,
even as I still yearn for a different sort of touch.
Remind me, Oh Bridegroom, that what I long for is but an
        earthly shadow
of the heavenly marriage that awaits.

The appetite of my flesh is an unfulfilling master,
but it points me to a truer desire: to be fully loved and fully
        known.
When I feel as if there is no way to endure this loneliness,
when all I crave is connection,
I will cry out to You,

trusting that You will meet me where I lack
and will make even this ache beautiful in its time.

Amen.

Psalm 25:16; 147:3 • Ecclesiastes 3:11 • Song of Solomon 8:4 • Mark 9:36–37 • Luke 8:43–48 • John 9:6; 13:1–17 • Hebrews 4:15

iv.

Relationships

Indulge in people. Give them more time than you should. Examine your one precious life, and see which names rise to the top, which faces dot your map. Remember who has thrown you a rope when you were drowning at sea. Consider who brings laughter out of you like steam curling from a boiling pot. Stand face-to-face, and let yourself be wounded by love. To spare your heart from decay, come close, even when it hurts, even when the possibility of rejection looms like a shadow. Thank God you have been cared for. Thank God you can care. Marvel at how you cannot know who you will meet next, who will change your life with their sudden and quiet entrance. Do not punish those who do not yet know you by heart, who cannot and will not know you as you know yourself. Then turn and cherish those who somehow *do* know you better than you know yourself—even if it's only One. Expand your definition of *soulmate*. Embrace the stickiness and messiness of fleshy relationships. Believe stubbornly that loneliness is not your inheritance.

A Liturgy for Friendship

Oh Christ, I rejoice in the deep satisfaction of friendship,
in the unceremonious familiarity of being known,
in the freedom to be no one other than myself.

Thank You for these signs of grace:
    the ease of conversation,
    the spontaneous eruption of laughter,
    the safety of silence,
    the relief of finding our way back to one another.

Let me never see friendship as commonplace
but as a rare and lavish gift.

As playful companions mature into confidants,
protect our growth with the cloud of Your presence.
Braid Yourself into our entwined hearts

so that the cords of partnership are not easily broken.
Teach us the way of covenant friendship
so that we may live by the words of Ruth—
Where you go I'll go; where you stay I'll stay.
Your people will be my people, and your God my God.

May we know the unselfish endurance of a friend who
    loves at all times.
May we willingly receive their wounds.
May ironclad honesty sharpen us,
sustaining our purest hearts,
smoothing our rough edges,
slicing away what keeps us from growth.

Just as You spoke face-to-face with Moses,
so we unveil our hearts to You in breathless wonder,
for You do not call us servants but friends.
We desire this friendship with You, too, Lord,
for even unto death have You loved us.

Oh Lord who extends the arm of kinship to all who desire it,
this is the greatest joy of friendship—
to freely abide in the company of one who loves us.
May we know this intimacy with You first and foremost
and with humble bravery allow ourselves to be known.

Amen.

Exodus 33:7–11 • Ruth 1:16–17 • 1 Samuel 18:1–5; 20 • Proverbs 17:17; 27:6, 17 •
Ecclesiastes 4:12 • John 15:15 • 2 Corinthians 3:18 • Philippians 2:8 • 1 John 3:1

A Liturgy for Feeling Butterflies Around Someone

This is new, Lord,
this fluttering of my stomach and flushing of my face.
I praise You for this person who has fully captured my
    attention.
The walls I built around my heart come down when they
    are near,
and composure feels impossible.
How frightening and wonderful to feel so exposed and
    alive.

Oh God, You know what I desire, but I will put words to it
    regardless:
I want to know this person more.
Will You awaken their desire to know me too?
Will You surprise me with the joy of intimacy?

Will You bring us together without me manipulating the
        crossing of our paths?
Time with this person would feel like a gift.

Keep me grounded even as my mind drifts, Oh Maker.
I do not want to get carried away with my own
        assumptions,
falling in love with an idea instead of a soul.
When my thoughts turn possessive, melt them into prayers
        for this person whom You love.
May I hold up my swirling thoughts like fireflies in a jar,
enjoying their light but examining them with distance,
intrigued but not consumed.

Oh Father, I am struck by this person's character and
        kindness,
their enthralling humanity,
and the depths of their mind and heart.
The mundane becomes magic with them.
But even if nothing blossoms between us beyond friendship,
I praise You for this stirring of my heart and this reminder
        that I was designed to adore.
If this is just a dim reflection of the affection You have for
        me, Oh Tender Pursuer,
and simply evidence that I was made to love and be loved,
then I thank You for this gift.

Amen.

Psalm 27:14 • Song of Solomon 2:5; 4:7; 5:10; 8:6 • Jeremiah 31:3 • Matthew 7:7–11 •
1 Corinthians 13:4–7 • 2 Corinthians 10:5

A Liturgy for Loving Someone Who Doesn't Love You Back

Oh Lord, I have opened my soul to another whose desire is
       not for me.
I have unlocked my heart
only to have it explored and discarded.
I have awakened to the melody of love
only to find myself singing it alone.

El Roi—God who sees—
look upon me now
in the desert of my disappointment,
in the valley of unrequited love,
in my separation from the one who has captivated my soul.
You are intimately aware of the sting of this loss.

I praise You for the one whom my heart is drawn to,
for You created them beautifully

and mysteriously complex.
What a gift they are to the world and to me,
even though they are unable to love me the way I love
        them.
I see who You have created them to be
and celebrate their future formation,
even though I will not be there as they flourish into their
        becoming.

Will You arise and comfort me, Oh Lord?
Will You receive me in this lonely night?
Be with me on my bed as I think of the one I love.
Be with me in the morning when I awake alone.
Be with me in the monotonous hours when I long for their
        presence,
for the simple effortlessness of their companionship.

Though this person will never know me the way I wish,
Your piercing gaze is fixed on my heart.
You run toward me with affection that never ends.
Your desires for me outnumber the stars in the sky.

Be for me the pure and loyal partner that they are not.
Show me that there is no one else but You.

Oh God,
my faithful companion,
my loyal lover,
set me as a seal upon Your heart when my worldly lovers
        abandon me.

I release my beloved with this blessing
and take hold of the hand of my Eternal Beloved:

To the soul that I hoped would be mine
and to the hands that do not hold me the way I wish.
To the current that draws you away from me
and to the path that I must continue down alone.
To the life that awaits you
and to anyone who will accompany you in the future.
To the years we will not share together
and to the lives we will never know.
I bless you on your journey, which will take you far from me.
I release you without asking for answers,
without needing the final word.
I love you too deeply to wish you harm,
and I leave you in the hands of God and others
who will care for you in the ways I wish I could.

God, go with me now as I turn in a new direction.
Light up my path with new and wondrous things.
With my broken heart tucked safely in the shadow of Your
        wings,
I lift up my eyes to a new and hopeful future.

Amen.

Genesis 2:18–25; 16 • Psalm 18:6; 46:1; 73:25–26; 91:4; 139; 147:3 • Song of Solomon
8:6 • Isaiah 42:10; 43:19 • John 3:16; 14:16–18

A Liturgy for Saying Goodbye

Oh Emmanuel,
You have birthed us into a world of goodbyes,
where going and coming are inevitable realities.

How do we prepare ourselves for this final moment of
        separation,
when we feel as though we would like to stay here
        forever?

Whether parting for a brief time
or mustering an indefinite farewell,
we pause to offer gratitude for the people, places, and sea-
        sons we leave behind.
We thank them for all they taught us,
even if the lessons were learned through struggle.
We honor the ache of separation,

for sad farewells mean we are relinquishing a good
        thing.

Oh God who is with us,
You know the pain of goodbyes all too well
and have felt the heavy ache of departure.
You left Your home in heaven to come to earth
and wept when Your dear friend Lazarus died.
You said a complicated goodbye to Peter, who abandoned
        You,
and a violent goodbye to Judas, who betrayed You.
You bid a tearful farewell to Your earthly mother
and offered up Your spirit to Your heavenly Father as You
        hung from the cross.
You are well acquainted with leaving.

May we say what needs to be said in these tender moments
        of parting
and have grace for all that is left unsaid.
May we wrap our memories in thick layers of gratitude
and trust that whatever comes next is held securely in Your
        hands.

Would You draw close to those who stay and those who
        leave?
For we must learn to adjust to life without one another.

For those of us who stay,
    would You quell our persistent worries
    and help us release the ones we love into Your
        protection?

We do not know what lies ahead for them
and fear that where they are going will not be as kind
as where they are coming from.

For those of us who leave,
would You guide us as we walk away from the familiarity of all we have known
and would You remain close to the loved ones we are
leaving behind?

With open hands and surrendered hearts,
we release what is past and journey toward unknown
horizons,
joyfully pressing on to discover what the next season of life
will hold.
May it be beautiful.
May it be better than before.
May an invisible strength come to us as we walk away
so that when we meet again, we will be more rooted and
established than ever.
May we look back on this goodbye and rejoice that we did
not hold on—grateful that we had the courage to
let go.

Oh God over all that is eternal,
parting is a temporary portion of life and a pain that will
not last forever.
May we take comfort in Your presence, which goes with us
and never leaves us,
and continuously call to mind Your resurrection,

for though we lose sight of one another for a short while,
Your eventual return is a promise of an eternal reunion.

Amen.

Psalm 139:5–15 • Isaiah 7:14 • Matthew 1:23; 26:47–50; 27:45–50 • Luke 22:54–62 •
John 6:38; 11:1–44; 19:25–27 • 1 Corinthians 15:51–57 • 2 Corinthians 4:16–18 •
Ephesians 3:14–19 • Philippians 3:13; 4:6–7 • Colossians 3:2; 4:2 • Revelation 21

A Liturgy for Showing
Kindness to Strangers

Today, Oh God, we will brush against many we do not yet
        know
in the places that mark our lives:
    offices,
    stores,
    traffic,
    street corners,
    lines.
Before stepping outside, we first ask for the unwarranted
        grace and self-forgetful love
to face the myriad and unpredictable temperaments of
        those around us.
Refresh our memory of the kindness You first extended to
        us
so that we may freely give it to those we meet.

Oh Lord, we do not know the weights others carry.
We do not know the heaviness with which a person got
      dressed this morning.
We do not see the grief that sits in their ribs like
      stones
or the joy we could so easily crush with any stray
      snideness.

May we walk and drive and move today as if the gospel
      were emblazoned on our chests,
as if every word and action were an ambassador for
      You.
May even our thoughts toward strangers be lovely,
rooted in humility and dressed in compassion.
Oh Faithful One, we know that generosity of heart will not
      make us poor
and that we will not lack anything after giving away kind-
      ness too liberally.

Today we will practice blessing our fellow sojourners
and will expect nothing in return except for the pleasure of
      our Messiah.
For if kindness is motivated only by hope of reward,
then how are we living like You, the One who humbled
      Himself to the point of death?
Purify our intentions and rid us of pride
so that all who encounter us may be surprised by our
      light,
paused by our patience,
touched by our tenderness,

and—above all, Oh God—seen by the One who created
their inmost being.

Amen.

Proverbs 11:17; 14:21 • Matthew 7:12 • Romans 12:10 • 1 Corinthians 13:4–8 • 2
Corinthians 5:20 • Galatians 5:13 • Ephesians 4:29, 32 • Philippians 2:8 • Colossians
3:12 • Hebrews 13:2 • 1 Peter 4:8

A Liturgy for Those Concerned
for Loved Ones

Oh High Priest who can sympathize with our weaknesses,
who had flesh-and-blood community of Your own,
You point our eyes to the lilies of the field
and the birds of the air
and remind us of Your detailed care.

Are not our loved ones more valuable than they?

How marvelous that You have given us others to love.
But, Lord, with this great love comes sorrow upon sorrow
as we confront each other's mortality
and bodies broken since the exit from Eden.

Remind us, Jesus, that for those who know You,
no sickness ends in death.
You always live to intercede for us,

so increase our faith to believe You do the same for our
      people.
Multiply our hours and energy so we can serve our families
      with an attitude of humility and selflessness,
and help us to love from a place without fear.
For we know this:
There is no fear in love.
There is no fear in love.
There is no fear in love.

We ache for those far away,
    whom we cannot embrace the way we want to.
We grieve for those we love who live alone,
    whose tears we cannot always dry.
We lament for those prone to sickness,
    whom we ask that You anoint with Your healing touch.

Oh God of mercy,
we mourn for those precious ones who do not know
      You yet,
in front of whom we will continually exalt Your praises and
serve and love ever deeper.

We rejoice in the knowledge that one day,
when sin and sickness and sorrow subside,
we will love and know one another as we are fully loved
      and known.
Until then, Gracious God, help us to care for our loved
      ones
wholeheartedly and freely,

trusting that the One who counts the sparrows will hold
them fast.

Amen.

Psalm 145 • Matthew 6:26–30 • Luke 8:49–55; 12:6–7 • John 11:4 • 1 Corinthians
13:12 • Philippians 2:1–11 • Hebrews 2:14–15; 4:15; 7:25 • 1 John 4:18* • Revelation
21:4

A Liturgy for Those Without
Words to Comfort Others

Teach me, Oh Father, how to care for Your beloved,
this person so dear who strains under a grief as wide and
　　　heavy as night.
I am familiar with the taste of an unassuaged affliction,
but I do not understand the dimensions and weight of this
　　　unique sorrow,
of this particular thorn stuck in their rib.
Clumsy and ill-equipped, I turn to You.

Platitudes and vain repetitions taunt my tongue,
but, Oh God of all comfort,
let no speech spill from my lips that will cut what must heal.
Help me, in my flailing desperation for a quick cure,
to not misconstrue Your character or misspeak what I
　　　know to be true.

Help me to not place a stake in false ground in my rush to
solve and mend.
May *"Everything happens for a reason"*
and *"Be strong"*
and *"God never gives us more than we can handle"*
die in my mouth before they reach the light of day.

Perhaps, Oh Christ, the tears You shed near Lazarus's
tomb
meant more to his aching sisters than any divinely inspired
speech.
Stir in me a mourning, Oh Jesus,
for what this person I love has lost,
and may I discern when silence is more medicinal than the
holiest of words.

Oh Father of compassion, call to my mind a record of
Your comfort in my own life,
of my own revelations in the valley.
Increase what I once received from You in the shadows
so that I can administer the same salve.

Astound me, Oh God, with the redemption of the
suffering I thought would crush me,
and repurpose the rescue I received from You in
the pit.
May the story of my own death and resurrection arouse
latent hope
in this person I have the honor of walking alongside,
and may my words be spare and my tenderness lavish.

Oh Lord, You alone know the depths of what has been
      stolen.

Give me unmerited insight so that I can tend to their
      bruised heart

in such a way that it feels as though You are near,

that You are the one holding their hand

and wiping their brow

and pulling them close.

Grant me the precious power of gentleness and nuance,

attention and grace,

and above all love, which binds everything together.

Amen.

Psalm 40:2 • Proverbs 15:4; 16:24; 25:11 • John 11:35 • Romans 8:26; 12:15 • 2 Corinthians 1:3–4 • Colossians 3:14

A Liturgy for Those Struggling to Forgive

Oh God of justice,
forgiveness feels like a journey in an unfair direction.
Blinded by fury and crippled with hurt,
I feel as though You have assigned me an impossible task.

How does one forgive when the debt is so great?
How does one pardon when the offense has cost life,
      health, or happiness?

When I look within myself,
    I find I lack the strength to extend the arm of mercy.
When I look within myself,
    I find I lack the compassion that would soften my heart
      to another.
When I look within myself,

I find that though I have been forgiven much, I am unable to forgive a little.

Oh Kind and Benevolent King,
You have set the example of pardon,
illuminating how it frees even the most hopeless of captives
free.
Hold space with me now as I mourn the wrong done and
pain inflicted,
for You do not ask us to overlook the severity of
wrongdoing
but desire us to release the perpetrator from their deserved
consequences—
to cancel the debt that they cannot pay.

No one has forgiven a greater debt than You, Lord,
and You are well acquainted with its price.
Help me cease the meticulous weighing of scales
and trust You with life's inevitable imbalances.
Help me remove the penalties that I have assigned to my
enemy
and place them in Your hand instead.

When everything in me rises up to seek revenge,
help me, Oh Lord, to fall back on Your strength.
When I cannot pacify my anger and resentment,
teach me, Oh King, the mystery of enemy love.
Give me compassion for the wounds that have driven my
adversary to wound,
and may forgiveness lay a foundation for both of our
healing.

Let me learn from You, Humble Teacher,
and grant me Your tender heart of kindness,
Your sharp eye for integrity.
Justice and mercy are twin rivers that run straight from
        Your heart,
and forgiveness will flow from a soul that trusts in Your
        sufficiency.

Where I judge, let me judge not.
Where I condemn, let me condemn not.
For I have received immeasurably more forgiveness than I
        will ever have to dispense.

My whole life flourishes out of the grace that You have
        given me, Lord.
May I dance in the delight of my own forgiven-ness,
seeking You for the grace to forgive others.
May I walk closely with You, Lord,
journeying down the path of mercy as You show me the
        way.

Amen.

Psalm 18:30; 52:8; 89:14 • Jeremiah 31:3 • Matthew 5:4, 7, 23–24, 43–48; 6:14; 7:1–3;
18:21–35 • Mark 11:25 • Luke 23:34–43 • John 13:34 • Ephesians 2:8; 3:14–19; 4:32 •
Colossians 2:13–14; 3:12

A Liturgy for Those
Contemplating a Breakup

When certainty gives way to confusion
and you lie awake at night in the swirling disarray of
     doubt,
look to the One in whom all wisdom is hidden.
When your feet feel unsteady on what you thought was
     immovable ground,
remind yourself—with tenderness—to pause in stillness
and fight the urge to flee without first counting the cost.

Do not be alarmed when the voice of doubt questions and
     probes,
when your relationship feels as if it has been strung under
     a harsh spotlight,
situated to be scrutinized and pulled apart.
You have not been left alone to muddle through your
     mind,

which heaves and churns like the sea.

Lean against your God, and confide in Him as you would
      a friend.

List what hurts and leave no detail out.

If His thoughts of you outnumber the grains of sand

and He knows the number of hairs on your head,

then surely He has a stake in this too.

As your ruminations turn to prayers,

let the Helper sift through the restless thoughts and churn-
      ing what-ifs,

winnowing what is real from what is not, as one separates
      wheat from chaff.

Where you have formed impossible expectations no one
      could meet,

    may you fix your eyes on Jesus, the only One who
      never falls short.

Where you have compared this flesh-and-blood person
      with the figment of your fantasies,

    may you repent for honoring your imagination more
      than them.

Where your mind has wandered to thoughts of a better
      partnership,

    may you clothe yourself in humility so you can rightly
      determine if this is the co-laborer you have been
      called to love.

Open your hands so you do not strangle this person with
      your uncertainty

but can rather love and serve them in the middle of it.

Remember the devastating power of a premature tongue,

and be slow to speak before it is time.

View this person not as a problem to be solved
but rather as a child of the Father who calls them beloved,
the apple of His eye.

Before you entwine yourself in covenant,
the freedom of choice and voluntary commitment can
	leave you dizzy,
as you feel tugged between two diverging paths: a life with
	this person or without.
Do not scorn yourself for this doubt, but remember your
	Savior,
who puts our fingers in His wounded side, helping us feel
	before we believe.
Unless you are held back by knowledge of transgression
or the looming sense of true incompatibility,
ride this doubt like a wave, trusting that the One who
	calmed the sea with a word
can also calm the stirring waters in you.

Amen.

Psalm 139:17–18 • Mark 4:35–41 • Luke 12:7 • John 20:24–29 • Romans 12:10 • Galatians 5:13 • Philippians 4:6 • Colossians 2:3 • Hebrews 12:2 • 1 Peter 5:5, 7 • James 1:19; 3:5

v.

Wonder

Wake up, and notice what is new, old, breathtakingly mundane. Notice the things that have been there all along, quietly waiting for you, happily continuing whether you saw them or not. Notice the way the light filters through specks of dust, the way dead things sparkle. Notice how the paint is peeling around the shutters, how everything is constantly in motion. Notice the skylights, the coffee grounds on the countertop, the shoes by the door, the fingerprints on the window—signs that the world is alive, that we are here together, that nothing stays the same. Notice that you are in the middle of your life. Notice that it is beautiful not because it is pleasant but because it is here. Because it exists. May you inhale with wonder, marveling at the miracle of being. May the plants on the windowsill, the books on the shelf, the candles on the mantel, the blankets on the bed, whisper hints of the life that is happening around you. May you look outward and upward, open-faced and openhearted, softened to all that awaits you.

A Liturgy for Those Looking for Joy

When the world expects sadness,
help us, Creator of light, to look for pockets of joy.
When the world is overwhelmed by darkness,
give us eyes to see little delights.
When the world is caught up in sensationalism,
help us speak of the hidden wonders we've
      discovered,
holding them up for others to see:
    the sacred stillness of the early morning,
    a quiet moment in the sun,
    small children laughing on scooters,
    trees bursting into bloom and lilies opening at the
      corner bodega.
These small joys reveal the truth of the world we
      live in.

No, there is not peace everywhere,
and all pain has not been removed.
But there are still people returning home,
　　voices that pray,
　　moments of forgiveness,
　　signs of hope.
We do not have to wait until all is well
to celebrate the glimpses of Your kingdom at
　　　　hand.

Let us not deny sadness
but transform it into fertile soil for joy.
Let us not deny the darkness
but choose to live in the light.
Cynics seek darkness wherever they go,
but joy is the mark of the people of God.
Help us discipline ourselves to choose joy,
for the reward is joy itself.
Help us renew our minds until they default to joy and not
　　　　fear,
for there is so much to frighten us.
Help us believe that the light can be trusted,
for there is so much darkness to mislead us.

Jesus, You are both the man of sorrows and the man of
　　　　complete joy.
Help us to hold both sorrow and joy in the ways You've
　　　　shown us.
Help us to remain in Your love
so that Your joy may be in us

and our joy may be complete.

Amen.

Note: This liturgy is inspired by Henri J. M. Nouwen, *The Return of the Prodigal Son: A Story of Homecoming* (New York: Doubleday, 1992).

Psalm 19:1–2; 22 • Isaiah 53:3–5 • John 1:5; 14:27; 15:9–11 • Romans 12:1–2 • 2 Corinthians 6:4–10 • Ephesians 5:8–14 • Philippians 4:4–9

A Liturgy for Those Who Haven't Belly Laughed Recently

Oh Christ, You have called us not servants but friends,
and is there any true friendship in which laughter is not the
glue that binds?
Much has been made of Your reputation as a man of
sorrows,
acquainted with grief,
but perhaps You are a God who rises from the grave
and eats breakfast on the shore with friends,
Your love-scarred side splitting with divine laughter,
sharing Your joy.

We confess that we have not obeyed the command
to be joyful always
and have forgotten that You exhort us
to become like little children,

careless in the care of You.
But like Sarah, we laugh only in our
barrenness and the cavern of disbelief.

We acknowledge the ever-widening gulf inside us—
    the stew of sin
    and sorrow
    and loneliness,
the pulse of Eden growing faint in our veins.
In the face of all that threatens, we ask for the
        impossible:
the loudest, fullest belly-deep laugh,
a gift from our scandalously playful Father.
Oh Lord, we ask that You help us to, as that poet
        suggests,
be joyful though we have considered all the facts.

Envelop us in divine hilarity.
Take our cynicism and trade it for delight.
Teach us the language of levity.
Grief is but an interlude, a shadow,
and joy is the truest substance for those who know You.
May we laugh deeply with those we love
and alone with You in the secret place.
For in this, we rejoice with the tongues of the redeemed
and practice resurrection.

There is no shame in laughing amid our sorrow,
for to laugh is to trust in You,
to believe that the rug we roll upon will not be pulled out,

to understand that the Author has given us a peek of eternity, and we know how the story ends.

Amen.

Note: The paraphrased quote in this liturgy is from Wendell Berry, "Manifesto: The Mad Farmer Liberation Front," in *New Collected Poems* (Berkeley, Calif.: Counterpoint, 2012).

Genesis 18:12 • Psalm 71:23 • Isaiah 53:3 • Matthew 6:26; 7:11; 18:3 • John 15:15; 21:1–14 • 1 Thessalonians 5:16–18 • Hebrews 12:2

A Liturgy for Commuting

Our days are composed of red lights and bus tickets,
train stations and highways—things so routine we take
     them for granted.
Perhaps these roads to and from home are not just a means
     to an end
but sacred ground, ripe with possibility.
Change the way I view my commute, Oh God,
and remind me that no time is wasted when I spend it on
     You.
Stir up joy in the secret place, Oh Lord, and release me from
     the apathy with which I have approached my travels.

I want the mundane to become fertile ground for meeting
     with You.
When my mind begs for stimulation and my ears itch to be
     filled,

help me determine when my headphones or radio will only
      drown out Your voice.
Grant me discernment to know when to choose silence and
      how to enjoy it.
May I indulge in stillness more than anything else.

Transform my commute into an experience of worship
      and attentiveness.
Draw my attention to the things I pass every day,
and use them as signposts to grow me in gratefulness and
      faith.

May each stop sign remind me to be still, trusting that You
      will work even when I pause.
May bridges remind me of the cross that spans the chasm
      between me and You.
May construction sites bring to mind how I, too, am a
      work in progress, always in the hands of my
      Maker.

Teach me how to rightly use these moments between desti-
      nations.
As I go, prepare and clean my heart, softening and steady-
      ing me for what lies ahead.
When I return, unburden me, restoring whatever I have
      lost to the day's demands.
May this vehicle feel less like an entrapment and more like
      a spacious place
where I can attune my ears to Your voice,
increasing my understanding of Your character and heart.

Above all, may I love You more and better because of my
commute, Oh Father.

Amen.

Exodus 14:14 • Psalm 18:19; 32:7; 46:10; 62:5 • 1 Thessalonians 5:18

A Liturgy for a Road Trip

We thank You, Oh Gracious God,
for these moments between our origin and our destination,
when we must learn to leave that which is behind
and wait with expectation for what lies ahead—
a symbolic and sacred discipline You delight to teach us.

Today, like every day, we do not depend on engines or tires
but rather on You, who protects us and commands angel
      armies to surround us.
We invite You to join us as a traveling companion,
covering our trip with the surety of Your presence and the
      comfort of Your person.
Be so near, Oh Friend, that it is as if You are filling a seat.

Oh Great Provider, we are thankful we do not travel this
      road alone.

Grant us space to be grateful for one another,
and give us words, filled with life, to say so.
Place psalms at the tip of our tongues to speak out loud.
Lead us into conversations that are both nourishing and
   selfless,
unafraid to enter new depths.
And when moments of silence inevitably come,
help us to make room for them without hesitation or fear,
for silence is often fertile ground for better things to grow.

As we voyage together along this road, we ask for a
   rekindling of wonder.
May the right songs play at the right time, stirring our souls
and creating in us a longing for the Source from which the
   beauty came.
May there be scenery outside our windows so lovely,
so surprising,
that we are overcome with affection for the One who
   created this world
that takes our breath away.
May even our bathroom breaks and gas station stops
be filled with a joy that does not make sense,
with a lightness of being we could not manufacture on our
   own.

May this car feel caught between heaven and earth,
a conduit for the grace we have been too busy to notice
   before.
Even in the lulls, may we, like Mary,
take time to ponder in our hearts the mystery of these
   things

so that when our pilgrimage finally draws to a close,
we will leave our vehicle as if exiting a sanctuary,
our faces shining because we have just encountered You.

Amen.

Exodus 34:29–35 • Numbers 6:24–26 • Proverbs 16:24 • Matthew 26:53 • Luke 2:19 •
Ephesians 5:19 • Philippians 3:13

A Liturgy for Those in Need
of a Good Cry

Oh Lord, there is no end to the chronic sorrow in our
        world,
and I have had my share.
Behind my wall of defense and mustered strength is a child
        who needs to cry,
to release tears as easily as breath,
to be unashamed in weakness and buoyed in trust.
So help me, Oh God, to liberate the floodgate I have
        clinched shut with my grown-up hands,
with my well-worn reflex to hold everything together.

Crying is surrender,
and I am ready to rest my burdens in the palms
of the One who has both designed tears and shed them,
who knows what it is to taste salt water before resurrection.

Oh Living Water, You do not provide a shortcut through
        grief and disappointment;
You do not fill the howling chasm in me with counterfeit
        joy;
You do not rush the welling of my eyes.
Instead, Oh Christ, You linger
and notice
and remember.

You say that You collect my tears in bottles,
that You keep a record of everything that moves me to the
        point of weeping.
Perhaps one day, after our glorious eternal reunion,
when tears are made obsolete and crying is but a memory
        lost,
You will still show me the glistening containers,
gesturing to the whole row of them and assuring me that
        not one drop escaped Your sight,
that each one was tallied with love in Your book.

Oh Lord, as I finally relent to what has been swirling
        inside,
may my tears not feel hollow as they fall,
devoid of substance,
but rather become the wet evidence that there is a spring
        in my heart I can draw from,
a well of life that can still be stirred.

I do not cry out of despair but rather out of confidence
        that when I am weak, You are strong.
May clarity come from this crying, Oh Father.

May You use these tears from my dust frame to melt what
      was clouding me,
to water what was shriveled and dried.
May I be blessed in my weeping, just as You promised.
Tonight I trust that You are both the man of sorrows and
      the creator of light,
so as I sow in tears, I know that tomorrow I shall reap with
      songs of joy.

Amen.

Genesis 1:3 • 2 Kings 20:5 • Psalm 56:8; 103:14; 126:5 • Isaiah 53:3 • Luke 6:21 • John 11:35 • 2 Corinthians 12:10 • Revelation 21:4

A Liturgy for Giving Thanks

How beautiful it is to clear the room for gratitude,
to be gentle with our memories and generous in our value
      of them.

One by one, we put these gifts on display,
like a parade of blessings that never end,
like a string of pearls—weighty with worth and
      shimmering with significance.

We sing a song of praise to You, Oh Giver of good things,
as we call to mind the ebenezers of Your faithfulness,
the emergence of Your unexpected provision,
the valleys where You did not forsake us.

As we remember, may we linger a little longer over what
      has brought us joy.

May we make a regular practice of recounting our days,
    our weeks,
    our years,
    so that not even the tiniest blessing slips through the
        cracks.
May we give thanks for the big and the small,
    for major breakthroughs and gentle breezes,
    for miraculous provision and momentary waves of
        delight.
For all of it is infinitely valuable.
All of it is evidence that we are meant to be alive.

May we seek first Your kingdom
and enjoy goodness to its fullest measure.
May we ask, seek, and knock without hesitation
and run to You with thanksgiving when You answer.
May our souls be happy in You,
for we have done nothing to deserve the bounty that we
        have received.

We offer a song of praise for the things that make us glad:
    Thank You for every moment You walked alongside us.
    Thank You for the moments we felt safe.
    Thank You for the memories that make us laugh.
    Thank You for meeting our needs and fulfilling our
        desires.

We offer a melody of trust for the things that we do not
        understand:
    Thank You for the discipline that taught us a better
    way.

Thank You for the loss that drew us into Your comfort.

Thank You for the waiting that brings us nearer to
Your heart.

Thank You for the unanswered questions that press us
to continue seeking.

We thank You for these gifts, God,

but more importantly, we pause to remember the Giver:

the One who withholds no good thing from those who
love Him,

the One who knows how to give good gifts to His
children,

the One who gives simply because He is generous,

the One who lavishes us with love,

the One who has purpose behind what He gives and
takes away.

Amen.

Job 1:21 • Psalm 16:9–11; 47; 84:11; 95:2; 98; 145:8 • Matthew 6:33; 7:7–11 • Luke
17:11–19 • Hebrews 2:12 • 1 John 3:1

A Liturgy for Generosity

When the stirring of charity has not been recently felt,
give away more than you can spare.
When the shrill voice of self-protection rings in your ear,
sacrifice and do it extravagantly.
Starve the lust to hoard,
and unclench your fists from what you cannot keep.

Determine to live in generosity—
unpack your bags and call it home.
Lend freely and often, ever mindful not of your
          reward
but of the One who first gave His whole self
and withheld nothing.
Do not count yourself exempt from the privilege of
          practicing
your Savior's self-denial.

Broaden how you define wealth,
and give from the hidden surplus of what you already
        have:
time, ability, words, space.
Discover where you're rich, and ask for grace to share.
Watch your subtraction become multiplication in the king-
        dom of God.
See how He nourishes others with your fish and
        loaves,
and rejoice when He receives the glory instead of
        you,
for this is true abundance.

May your left and right hands become strangers—
lean fully into the beauty of anonymity, for you are not un-
        seen by the One who counts.

Consider creation, and see how the sun does not spare
        light,
how the flowers of the field withhold no beauty,
how rivers feed oceans and lose nothing.
If this is how nature reflects the open hand of her
        Creator,
then how much more shall you, His chosen *imago Dei*?
Picture the face of Your Father, who does not burden you
        with the law
but rather invites you into the lavish freedom of cheerful
        giving,
the light-footed spontaneity that comes only through a life
        untethered to possession.

May sacrifice begin to feel more like worship
and taste more like delight.

Amen.

Psalm 41:1–3 • Proverbs 11:24–25 • Matthew 6:3, 19–20; 10:42 • Mark 8:36 • Luke
21:1–4 • John 6:1–13 • 2 Corinthians 9:6–8 • Philippians 2:1–11 • 1 Timothy 6:17–19
• 1 John 3:16–18

A Liturgy for Those
Who Are Homesick

Here sits the longing as familiar as the back of my hand,
the ache for both the home I had and the home I have.
I am pulled between places,
tugged by the knowledge that I cannot be wholly tethered
      both here and there.
Oh Lord, it is a wonder this divided heart does not shatter.

My yearning is greater than geography and beyond brick
      and mortar—
what I crave is the surety that I am rooted in the right
      place,
the assurance that I have not chosen to grow where You
      have not planted me.
Oh God of Israel—
Lord of those who once left home in pursuit of a greater
      one—

teach me how to carry this split love.
Help me see the generosity You have shown
in giving me multiple places to belong.

It is not strange to know the pain of a paradise lost.
Our story began with a home and ends with a home—
we live between Eden and New Jerusalem,
straddling what has passed and what is to come.
My homesickness is an inherited one,
a visceral reminder that this is but a rented world.
Help me see, Oh Father, that these homes I long for with
      my whole self
are but faint tastes before the true feast to come.

Where can this nomadic body move from Your presence?
Teach me how to truly live,
how to count all earthly addresses as a loss
because of the surpassing worth of knowing You.
Assure me, Oh Christ, that You are my surest respite,
the place in which I can always settle, always return.
And as I make You my dwelling place, remind me how—
      glory upon glory—
You also make Your home in me.

Amen.

Genesis 12:1–5 • Psalm 91:1–2; 139:7–10 • Isaiah 32:18 • John 14:2 • Ephesians 3:17 •
Philippians 3:8

vi.

Mystery

WHEN THE NAGGING NEED for understanding overtakes you, look not for the right answers but for the right questions. Allow yourself to pause. Linger gently in the moments when breath catches in your throat. Hang on to every word—or perhaps forget words entirely. Now is an opportunity to explore the unknown, to raise a curious eyebrow at the unexplained. What is there to be learned in waiting? What insight does the ache of mourning impart? And those empty spaces we wish were filled—what do they have to say? Observe nameless angst with curiosity. Examine desire with generosity. Be gentle with grief. Step across the threshold of easy answers, and go deeper into that realm children seem to find with ease. Do not retreat from questions that feel impossible to answer, but with eyes wide open, allow the mystery to lead you to truths you did not know existed. May you be compelled by divine wisdom, for it is available to all who seek.

A Liturgy for Waiting for
a Dream to Come True

How long, Oh Lord, how long
will I cry with empty hands?

Like Hannah, who wept in Your house
    and begged for a child,
I pour out my longing before You,
aching for a gift that I do not have and may never receive,
carrying the invisible burden of the not yet,
asking with my soul laid bare,
Do You care about my dreams, God?

We are all stories in search of an ending,
descendants of pioneers and pathfinders,
destined for a denouement we cannot comprehend.
But the cost of dreaming feels like a price I can no longer
        pay.

With a trembling voice and a mind prone to doubt,
I say in faith, *I trust You, Lord.*
You know the shape of my sorrow and the anguish of my
      soul.
You measure my heart heaviness in the center of Your
      palm.
You also make everything beautiful in its time,
masterfully orchestrating symphonies of purpose for Your
      children.

I confess that I do not always know what is best for me,
yet if it seems good to You, Oh Lord,
grant my petition and end my waiting.
But if I desire something that will one day bring harm,
gently but firmly protect me from myself.

May I trust that there is wisdom and intention behind
      every delay,
for Your ways are not my ways; Your thoughts are not my
      thoughts.
Let me never think that You do not care about my
      dreams
or that a dream delayed is evidence of Your cruelty or
      punishment,
for You are a generous Father who does not withhold any
      good thing from His children.

Remind me how brave it is to hope, to dream,
to ask You for the same thing again and again.
Let me trust that the doors You open

and the doors You keep closed
are all necessary for my long-term flourishing.

As I draw near to You in the waiting,
align my desires with Yours,
and give me a vibrant vision for thriving.
May I delight in the nearness of Your presence
and enjoy the easy yoke of partnership with You.

Ah, Sustainer of hope,
let me never grow weary of wishing,
but keep my heart soft to dream again.
Astonish me.
Delightfully bewilder me.
Exhilarate and confound me
until I surrender to the relief of my own smallness,
until I am rendered speechless with new and beautiful
    realities.
Teach me a marvelous new song,
and hold me securely in Your deepest peace.

While I wait,
may I boast in Your nearness,
for I am proud of the sufficiency of Your grace.
May I patiently endure,
for those who wait on the Lord will renew their strength.
May I worship You without restraint,
for Your open hand satisfies the desire of every living
    thing.
May I consider the lilies,

for You have clothed me with more beauty and splendor
> than they.
And may I wait expectantly,
for You will surely provide more than I could ask, seek, or
> imagine.

Amen.

1 Samuel 1 • Psalm 8; 13; 16; 31; 33:20–22; 39:7; 56; 84:11; 115:1; 139; 145:16 • Ecclesiastes 3 • Isaiah 40:29–31; 55:8–9 • Habakkuk 3:17–19 • Matthew 6:28–30; 11:28–30 • 2 Corinthians 12:9 • Ephesians 3:20

A Liturgy for a Disappointment

We pause and hold unashamed space
for these days beset with disappointments we could not see
      coming
and reminders of what could have been.
Oh Loving Maker, restore our belief that You redeem what
      is lost
but also that our grief is safe with You
and that lamenting is not a waste of our precious time.

Oh Christ, You do not scorn our disappointment
but rather remind us that You are a God who was enrobed
      in human flesh
and has felt salt run down Your own divine face.

Oh, how glorious! How wonderful to have a Savior who understands!

Hope deferred makes our hearts sick,

so we ask that You remind us, Oh Sweetest Friend,

that what we grieve—

the canceled event,

the lost job,

the health of a loved one or ourselves,

the broken relationship,

the end of a project that stirred our hearts—

was never the source of our hope to begin with.

You say we are blessed when we mourn, for we shall be
          comforted.

Come near and be our deepest consolation now, Father.

Tend to our grief-stricken hearts, and lead us into the
          warmth of Your relief,

the tenderness of Your Word,

the marrow-deep peace of Your presence,

the greater intimacy we can enjoy with our suffering Savior.

We mourn the loss and death of our good dreams, Oh
          Creator,

and ask that You resurrect them if Your gracious will al-
          lows.

But for now, we look toward the day

when every tear will be gone

and we will meet You, the One in whom all our hope
          resides.

Amen.

Deuteronomy 30:3 • Psalm 25:5; 42:11; 119:50 • Proverbs 13:12 • Matthew 5:4; 26:38
• John 11:33–36 • Revelation 21:4

A Liturgy for Empty Space

Our lives are littered with pockets of emptiness,
chambers of time and space,
crying out for meaning,
longing for purpose,
aching for something to fill the void.

We fill and refill broken cisterns:
    the groaning hollow of our empty stomachs,
    the unexpected gap of canceled plans,
    the nagging nothingness of boredom,
    the gaping wound of severed relationships—
    those vacant places a special person used to fill.

Oh Lord,
fill these innumerable empty spaces
with the satisfying substance of Your Spirit.

Be welcomed into our wondrous unknowns.
Surprise us with gladness when You meet us in the
        unfamiliar deserts of lonely nights and unexplored
        seasons of life.

There is a richness of relationship to be found here,
for wandering the wilderness is essential to our journey of
        coming to You.

Fill what is hollow with Your presence
until we experience the fullness of joy.
Reveal the new creations that flourish
when they are given room to grow.

The intensity of our yearning terrifies us,
but You remain close,
guiding us through the pathless expanse.

We come to You thirsty, Oh Lord;
teach us to drink Your living water.

Let emptiness invite us into fathoms of meaning
and awaken our senses to unseen banquets.
Let the vacuity of a moment excite us,
for there may be more in store for us than what we
        immediately perceive.

May we have the courage to remain where there is no
        visible foothold,
for when we have nothing to cling to,
we are held even still.

Most of all, let us simply allow this space to be empty,
for emptiness is not lack to You.

Amen.

Psalm 16; 121:5 • Isaiah 44:3 • Jeremiah 2:13 • John 4:10; 7:37–38 • Romans 8:26;
15:13 • 1 Peter 1:3

A Liturgy for the Fear of Missing Out

Come, Oh Limitless God, into the gap between us and the
        places we long to be.
Though our spirits were made for eternity, our bodies are
        bound up in time,
and the finality of the present can feel like too much to
        bear.

We long to rearrange time and space, chronology and
        cosmos,
to sample the endless array of opportunities before us.
We ache with curiosity to peer into the moments we can't
        see.

Perhaps this is our greatest act of trust—
to release all that we will never experience
and trust that being where we are is enough.

Oh Lord, may we not be afraid of missing out,
worrying that our lives may somehow diminish in value;
may we not be afraid of missing our purpose,
toiling frantically as though we were already behind.
But may we trust the pace of our lives to You,
for though we plan our steps, You infuse them with
      meaning.
We trust You, Oh God, with all that we will never know.

May we embrace the sacred rhythm of choice,
perceiving when it is time to say yes
and discerning when it is time to say no.
May we not be afraid to forego an event, an assignment, or
      a relationship
if it is not the best use of our time, our gifts, or our energy.
Grant us the humility to know when our presence is not
      required,
and open our eyes to Your direction if we need to change
      course.
May we hear Your voice behind us saying,
This is the way; walk in it.

So here are our bodies, Lord.
Here are our calendars.
Here are our careers and accomplishments.
We are Your workmanship.
Like clay, we are the malleable materials of Your hand.
Form us now into handcrafted vessels,
equipped to complete the good works You have prepared
      for us.
All that we have done and have left undone is Yours.

Everywhere we go and desire to go is Yours.

May we release ourselves from the burden of infinite
    unknowns

and uncover the riches of joy hidden deep inside hearts of
    contentment.

Amen.

Psalm 16:5–6 • Proverbs 3:5–6; 16:9 • Ecclesiastes 3 • Isaiah 30:21;* 64:8 • Matthew 5:37; 6:33 • Luke 12:27–34 • Romans 12:1 • Ephesians 2:10; 5:15–17 • Philippians 1:6; 4:11–13

A Liturgy for Waves of Grief

Oh Lord, You know the rise and fall of my grief.
You sustain my heart as it collapses in sorrow.
You uphold my body under the weight of all I have lost.
I come to You as a broken vessel,
leaking with lament.
How long until these cracks are mended?
How long until these waves subside?

Crippled by the current of catastrophe,
I limp to You for healing.
Wrecked by the flood of disaster,
I reach out for You.
You, who are no stranger to sadness,
You, who are well known by grief,
acquaint me now with these inevitable companions

so I may learn the cadence of their current
and gracefully ride the rhythm of their tide.

Surely You are with me now,
bearing this burden and shouldering my sorrow.
One word from You silences the raging sea,
and the sound of Your voice calms the fiercest storm.
Though I am caught in the winds of a hurricane,
Your love is the lighthouse that keeps me from crashing
   upon the rocks.

Though You slay me, I will hope in You.
Though I wander in this dark valley, I will remind my soul
   of Your love.
Through tears, I will call this truth to mind and have
   hope:
The steadfast love of the Lord never ceases;
His mercies never come to an end;
they are new every morning.

Oh Compassionate One,
as I pour out my grief,
You pour out Your love.
This is the relationship I have with You,
my rock and my redeemer.

Show me how to suffer well.
Teach me to consider joy.
Help me bravely face wave after wave,
for You have promised to face them with me.

Out of the anguish of my soul will come gladness.

Out of the desolation of my body will come restoration.

Out of the grim black of night will come the dawning of
joy.

I will look forward to the day when You will wipe away
every tear.

I will practice remembering that You make all things new.

But for now, Oh Great Comforter, steady me,

for though the waves crash, they will not crush me.

I am holding on to You.

Amen.

Job 13:15 • Psalm 19:14; 31; 56:8; 89:9 • Isaiah 43:1–2; 53 • Jeremiah 8:18 • Lamentations 3:22–23, ESV;* 3 • Romans 5:5 • 2 Corinthians 4:7–12 • 1 Thessalonians 4:13–14
• James 1 • Revelation 21:4–5

A Liturgy for Those Who Don't Know How to Help

We have placed the weight of the world's suffering upon
       our shoulders
instead of Yours, Oh Deliverer.
We are mired in hesitation and overwhelmed by stagnancy.
Our nation groans with need,
suffering multiplies by the hour,
and it is not the call of Your children to ignore our
       neighbors' cries.

Where our understanding falters,
where our knowledge dwindles,
where our expertise ends,
Oh Lord, You meet us there.
Your Word is a lamp to our feet and a light to our path
when we cannot see the next right step.
Oh Loving God, You have said this is Your will:

to be joyful always,

to pray continually,

to give thanks,

to do justice,

to love kindness,

to walk humbly with You.

Our portion is You and Your redemptive work.

Show us how to be Your ambassadors to this hurting
world.

Teach us how to use our hands and resources when words
fall short.

Define Your ministry of reconciliation for each of us, Jesus.

Bless those who have not the time to feel helpless:

those on medical front lines,

those teaching their children,

those caring for the vulnerable,

those turning the gears of our cities.

Oh Author and Perfecter of our faith, You use us

to write a beautiful story amid crisis.

As parts of Your body, appointed by the same Spirit,

we do not receive Your grace in vain,

and we trust we have everything we need to abound in
every good work.

Amen.

Psalm 3:8; 16:5–8; 119:105 • Lamentations 3:22–24 • Micah 6:8 • Mark 12:30–31 •
John 13:12–17 • 1 Corinthians 13:8 • 2 Corinthians 5:15–21; 6:1; 9:8 • 1 Thessalonians
5:16–18 • Hebrews 12:2

A Liturgy for Letting Go
of Your Younger Self

Oh God who is not bound to time,
we know ourselves in pieces
at various ages and evolving stages—
every point in our lives
shaping us into whom we were meant to be.

We are constantly emerging,
greeting a new self with every passing year,
shedding old skin and exploring a person we do not yet
      know.

Oh Lord, when it seems as though the loveliness of our
      youth is slipping away,
may our security not slip along with it.
May we not punish ourselves for changing

or attempt to shrink back into the person we used to know.
For it is good and right to outgrow our youth,
to continuously increase in knowledge and wonder,
to leave behind the layers that no longer fit.

May we grieve the loss of the people we once were,
knowing they are not eternally lost but simply fading out
      of the present.
May we honor even the self we disliked,
trusting that You redeem the unpleasant colors of the
      past.
May we expand and mature with bravery,
fulfilling all the potential You have placed within us.
May we generously befriend who we are becoming.

Only You, Lord, see our full selves from beginning to end,
      uninterrupted by time.
When You say the old is gone and the new has come,
You are referring not to age or time but to our eternal
      identities,
unchanging and preserved by Your Holy Spirit.

It is safe to grow old,
for our younger selves are remembered and treasured by
      You.
No matter our age, our identity in Christ never changes,
for we are reconciled to You.

So we release the younger selves that brought us this far
and welcome the new selves that will take us on from here

as we wait for the resurrection of our bodies
and behold new wonders with every passing day.

Amen.

Psalm 90:2; 92:12–14; 139:15–16 • Proverbs 16:31; 20:29 • Luke 2:52 • John 11:25–26
• Romans 6:4; 8:28 • 2 Corinthians 1:22; 4:16; 5:17–18 • Ephesians 2:10 • Philippians
3:13 • Hebrews 5:14–6:1 • 2 Peter 3:8

A Liturgy for Those Who Can't Be Good Enough

Oh Lord, deficiency is in our marrow,
and decay is in our bones.
We have attempted godliness
and been found wanting.

Your faultless eyes scan the earth,
searching for one who understands,
seeking someone who hungers after You.
But no one is righteous; no, not one.
No one understands;
no one seeks You.
We all, like sheep, have gone astray,
each of us has turned to our own way,
and we are unaware of just how far
from Your goodness we have wandered.

We hardly have words, Oh God,
to convey the depths of our spiritual poverty
and our insufficient ability to earn Your favor.
If the wages of sin are death,
then we have justly earned our end.

Help us, Lord, for we do not know the way to
      life.
We have the desire to do what is right
but lack the ability to carry it out.
Who will save us from our destiny of death?

Thanks be to God through Jesus Christ our
      Lord!
He is merciful
   though we fall short,
gracious
   though we were His enemies,
slow to anger
   though we repeatedly stray,
abounding in love
   though we deserve condemnation,
relenting from disaster and releasing us from a debt that
      we cannot pay.

Holy Father, we cling to Your character, of more worth
      than gold.
We accept Your grace and the honor of being Your
      ambassadors.
We treasure the good news that sinners can be reconciled
      to You.

Like the thief who hung alongside You on the cross,
remember us, Lord, when You come into Your kingdom.
We cannot reach You by ourselves,
but You bridge the gap between us with Your body and
blood.

The old has gone; the new is come.

Amen.

Psalm 53:1–3 • Isaiah 53:4–6* • Jonah 3–4 • Matthew 5:3; 18:23–27 • Luke 23:39–43
• John 8:1–11 • Romans 3:10–24; 6:23; 7:15–25 • 2 Corinthians 5:17–21

A Liturgy for the Aftermath of a Crisis

When the immediacy of catastrophe has passed
and we blink awake into lives we once lived,
help us, Repairer of ruins, to pick up the pieces
of our families,
of our homes,
of ourselves.

We come to You in this settling of dust,
mourning all we have lost,
holding shards of memories,
shouldering trauma that has changed us in ways we do not
        yet understand.

Would You walk this road of recovery with us,
speaking peace to our fragile, forgetful minds,

refreshing us with the truth that we are always sustained by
      Your hand?

May we look to You for the wisdom and skills necessary
to rebuild the ruins that are in front of us,
and may the restoration of our lives lead others to put
      their faith in You.
May we not fear the next disaster
but trust that all authority under heaven and earth is
      Yours,
for You have promised to be with us always—even to the
      end of the age.

As we move forward into less turbulent times,
would You remind us of the intensity with which we clung
      to You in our hour of need
and the urgency with which we depended on You?

May our hearts burn within us as we recall how closely
      You walked with us,
and may we continue to acknowledge our need for You.

Yes, Keeper of lifetimes,
You have made our days a few handbreadths,
and surely we are mere guests on this earth,
temporarily passing through until death awakens us to our
      eternal existence with You.
Help us to maintain this perspective
and remember that You hold the foundations of the world
      steady.

In times of crisis and in times of peace,
You do not change.
We acknowledge that calamity will come again,
but tragedy is not the end of the story for Your children.

We look forward to the promise of eternal Eden,
when the dwelling place of God will be among us,
when our pain will be rendered a former thing,
when the days of mourning will completely pass away.

Together we say, "We trust in You.
Our times are in Your hands."

Amen.

Nehemiah 1–3 • Psalm 31; 39; 40; 55:22 • Isaiah 43:18–19; 46:4; 61:1–7 • Matthew 28 • Mark 16 • Luke 24:13–49 • John 16:33 • Hebrews 13:20–21 • Revelation 21

vii.

Confession

FEEL HOW THE WORDS rise from within, catching in your throat, coming up for air. We cannot hide forever. What has grown larger in shadows is ready to greet the day. Believe that what you feared most will appear small in the light and may never come to pass. Indulge in confession, and toss off the fig-leaf camouflage you wear. Exchange your shame for freedom, and trust the One in whom there is no darkness at all. Liberate yourself from the rubber chains you thought were metal. See how easily they slide off. Let the ones you trust unlock them for you, and notice how much closer you become. Confessing will untangle the knots in your chest, will help you breathe again, will help you love with an unobstructed heart. Say the words that rise from within. Be unburdened at last.

A Liturgy for Perfectionists

God of immeasurable perfection,
all we can see is all we are not.
We are haunted by the sense that we will never
    measure up,
consumed by the belief that we will never be
    enough—
so meet us here in our helplessness.

We are mysteries unto ourselves, Lord,
demanding standards we are incapable of
    keeping,
motivated by a desire to do what is good
yet lacking the ability to carry it out.
The world tells us that we are enough,
but deep down, we fear that we are not.

If we cannot shake this sense that there is one right way,
if we detect within ourselves a compulsion to be perfect,
perhaps this is from You—
    echoes of whom we were meant to be but are not,
    whispers of the eternity You have placed in our hearts,
    inklings of whom You will one day resurrect us to be.

Our spirits cry out for perfection,
    for wholeness,
    for our wrongs to be forever righted,
    for our every failure to come untrue—
but we were never meant to bear the burden of our own
        salvation.

You, Spotless Savior,
are the only one strong enough to bear our faults.
You, Lamb of God,
are the one who takes away the sins of the world.
Your way is always the right way.
Your heart is always pure.
Your love is always unsullied.
Your grace is always sufficient to provide for us in our
        shortcomings.

Why would we ever seek perfection in ourselves
when perfection belongs to You alone?
You lived the faultless life that we could not.
You died the rebel's death that we deserve.

Thank You, Author and Perfecter of our faith,
for revealing our tendency toward perfectionism,

for to be caught in weakness is a mercy.

Your kindness leads us to repentance,

and we repent now for our countless attempts to be our
own saviors.

Let us never think, Oh God, that You expect us to be
perfect in our own strength,

but rather, strengthen us in our weakness.

You are the way and the truth and the life.

Let the pain of our imperfections be a gentle reminder of
our need for You.

Amen.

Deuteronomy 32:4 • Psalm 18:30; 19:7–14 • Ecclesiastes 3:11 • John 1:29; 14:6 • Romans 2:4; 3:23; 7:15–20 • 1 Corinthians 15:50–58 • 2 Corinthians 12:9–10 • Hebrews 12:2 • 1 Peter 2:24

A Liturgy for Jealousy

As fear enchants us with stories of scarcity
and half-formed narratives of another's success,
we are lured away from contentment,
only to be abandoned in the valley of disappointment.

How human of us, Lord,
to cherish what we do not have
and to glorify another's abundance while losing sight of
      our own.

We see the varied riches of those around us:
    abundant wealth,
    effortless beauty,
    compounding success,
    open doors of opportunity.

We even envy our brothers' and sisters' faith,
coveting their unique intimacy with You,
craving their peace that appears to go deeper than ours.

We have seen this avarice since the dawn of time,
when a lust for knowledge led to strife in Eden,
a thirst for power led to the fall of Babel,
a craving for comfort led the Israelites to fantasize about
    Egypt
rather than trust Your provision in the wilderness.

Help us, Lord, for this awareness of our lack can make us
    lose our way.
Satisfy us with Your Spirit so that we may live as people
    who are already full.
May we not be greedy for the gifts You have given to
    others
but be overflowing with gratitude for the portions You have
    allotted to us,
trusting that even what we lack may be Your greatest kind-
    ness to us.

May we bring our jealous desires to You
and humble ourselves to see from Your perspective,
for one person's blessing does not equal our deficiency.

May we see one another not as rivals
but as essential elements to the body of Christ.
And when we encounter a life we do not have but
    desperately want,

tend to our grief and hold us close,

for it is not the desire that brings us harm

but the belief that possessing it will give us greater
       self-worth.

Oh God of divine jealousy,

You desire us with an all-consuming love,

but where human jealousy is dangerous,

Your divine jealousy is pure.

It is right that You should desire us for Yourself,

for to know You is what we were created for,

and to love You is how we are made whole.

Amen.

Genesis 3; 11:1–9 • Exodus 20:2–6, 17; 34:14 • Numbers 11:4–6 • Psalm 95:6; 107:9 •
Proverbs 21:26 • Lamentations 3:24 • Matthew 18:1–5 • Luke 22:24–30 • John 15:9–12
• Romans 12:2–3; 13:9 • 1 Corinthians 12:12–27 • Colossians 3:5 • Hebrews 13:5–6 •
James 4:10 • 1 John 2:15–17

A Liturgy for Those Who
Feel Self-Conscious

Oh Lord, I am consumed with thoughts of myself:

    the way my body moves,

    the way my clothes fit,

    the sound of my own voice,

    the awareness of being watched by others.

How strange and unnatural it is to wonder how we are
      regarded.

Let me not assume, Oh Lord, that I can see what others see.

For I will never experience my own presence.

    I will never observe the way my eyes light up when I
        speak of what I love.

    I will never hear my voice through someone else's ears.

    I will never fully understand another person's percep-
        tion of me

    or look through the lens of their own experience.

Let me entrust who I am and how I am seen to You,
    for it is an act of faith to simply be myself.
Let me take up less space in my own head
    and instead be filled with thoughts of You.
Let me regard myself with the measure of grace that You
        extend,
        for when I feel judged, it only means that I judge
        myself.
Let me cease to evaluate from a human point of view
    but behold the new creation You have made.

Oh my soul, instead of fixating on yourself,
    fix your eyes on the Author and Perfecter of your faith.
When you are afraid of not being enough—faint not,
    for your inner self is being renewed with every passing
        day.
When you are preoccupied with what your eyes can see,
    call to mind the greater realities of God,
    for everything of the earth is temporary,
    but the unseen riches of His kingdom are eternal.

No eyes are set on me in the way that I fear,
    but I am held by the adoring gaze of the One who
        fashioned my heart.
No one's opinion can determine my worth,
    for my heart is fixed on a firm foundation.

Your steady love, Oh Lord, has captivated my attention.
Your mysterious wonders arrest my thoughts.
Your sovereign steadiness frees me from the anxiety of self-
        promotion.

With every step I take, may I plant my feet securely,
knowing that I am rooted and grounded in love;
may I walk with a sustained fearlessness,
for the Mighty One is with me;
may my countenance be effortlessly radiant,
for I will never be put to shame.

Amen.

Psalm 18:35–36; 34:5; 36:5–12; 37:23; 75:7; 119:133; 139 • Zephaniah 3:17 • Matthew 6:33; 7:24–27 • 1 Corinthians 13:12 • 2 Corinthians 4:16–18; 5:16–17 • Galatians 1:10 • Ephesians 3:17 • Philippians 4:8 • Hebrews 12:2 • James 4:12

A Liturgy for Those Battling Fear

Do not be afraid, Your angels proclaimed to those shaking
      shepherds,
and You whisper the same to us, generation after
      generation.
But disease ravages our world,
heartbreak turns commonplace,
and nameless grief settles deep in our bones.
Is it any wonder we tremble so easily?

You remember that we are made of dust and breath
and how our unnaturally natural tendency is to cower in
      the dark places of our minds,
pointing fingers at one another,
forgetting the shadow of safety You offer under Your
      wings,
wide enough to hold us all.

Our groaning is not hidden from You, Oh Holy Father.
Do not ignore our weeping cries
and quaking knees
and besieged hearts.
You alone hold power to pull us from the miry pit,
for fear has stolen our ladder and we cannot escape.

How long, Oh God?
When will we see Your goodness in the land of the living?

Remind us, Jesus, that You lay sleeping in the boat
in the middle of the storm at sea.
You are neither surprised nor distressed by the mounting
    chaos.
You are not a God who panics.

Oh Christ, who defeated the sting of death upon the cross,
    be near
and calm the sea within us with one word so that we may
    then comfort others
with the same comfort You give to us.
Out of Your loving-kindness You do not condemn our fear
but rather call us into something far more magnificent:
wild, glorious trust in the One who holds the whole world
    together.

Amen.

Genesis 2:7 • Psalm 13; 27:3, 13; 36:7; 38:9; 40:2; 91:1–4; 103:14 • Mark 4:35–41 •
Luke 2:8–10* • 1 Corinthians 15:55–57 • 2 Corinthians 1:3–4

A Liturgy for a Lonely Evening

Meet me here, Oh Lord, while I am alone,
while the house is quiet,
while I—at last—have the space to listen for Your reassuring voice.
May the noise of the day fall away.
May the quiet rhythm of my breath dissolve my anxious
thoughts.
May this plentitude of silence clarify Your still, small voice.

Sometimes I forget that You are my shepherd—
that You have taught my heart Your native tongue.
Sometimes I forget that I lack nothing—
that my soul is a cup that overflows.
Teach me, again, to listen for Your voice,
which beckons me to cease striving and know that You are
God.

Eliminate my dread of loneliness,

for I do not face this silent moment alone.

Let solitude show me new things.

Let isolation whisper wonders.

Let the thoughts I have been avoiding come out into the
open,

and may whatever is stuck in my heart be processed without shame.

If I need to cry, let me cry.

If I need to laugh, let me laugh.

If I need to rest, let every muscle relax and all tensions be
released.

Though I have no plans,

this night is not wasted.

Though I am not surrounded by companions,

I am not forgotten.

Carry me away to Your green pastures.

Walk with me beside Your still waters.

Refresh my soul with the safety of Your company,

and help me bear the weight of my present aloneness.

Meet me here, Oh Lord, while I am alone.

This vacant time is a gift,

ready and waiting to be filled with You.

Amen.

1 Kings 19:9–12 • Psalm 23; 46:10; 145:5 • Matthew 28:20 • John 10:27–28 • Colossians 3:17

A Liturgy for Those Who Feel Forgotten

Oh God who sees me inside and out,
I groan with an insatiable appetite for attention,
for an existence drenched in significance.
I want to live a life that is seen, known, and admired—
a life so big that no one could forget me.
I am predisposed to seek reassurance from others,
but the truth is, I will not always be remembered by others
      in the way that I want.

Oh Lord, when obscurity feels like too much to bear,
when loneliness threatens to crush me,
when I fear that my value is slipping away,
let me run with tears in my eyes back to You.
Meet my downcast gaze with Your tender regard.
Remind me that I am never ever alone.

When I am unseen by others,
it is easy to believe that I am worth forgetting.
But before I knew what it was to be loved or unloved,
You engraved me on the palms of Your hands.
Like a nursing child with its mother,
I am not forgettable to You.

When I feel utterly forsaken, You embark on a relentless
    search for me.
You run toward me when I am still a long way off.
You rejoice over me more than the ninety-nine that were
    never lost.
You put my found-ness on display and clothe me with
    honor.

As Your dearly beloved child,
I give this sense of my own insignificance to You.
Teach me the presence and purpose of my soul, Oh
    God,
and sing to my heart the song of belonging.

Let me not fear when others fail to notice me,
for humans can be fickle when it comes to love.
Rather, let me bear this truth in mind and take
    courage:
Your eyes are fixed on the weakest of sparrows,
and the hairs of my head do not escape Your care.

Let me seek Your never-ending companionship
and call to mind Your everlasting pursuit.

Because You do not forget me, Oh Lord,
and You never will.

Amen.

Psalm 131:2; 139:1–2; 145:18–19 • Ecclesiastes 1:1–11 • Isaiah 49:13–16 • Lamentations 3:21–23 • Zephaniah 3:17 • Matthew 6:26 • Luke 12:6–7; 15 • Colossians 3:12

A Liturgy for Those Who Feel Like Something Bad Is About to Happen

When unnamable dread creeps into our bones
and impending doom looms large in our minds,
teach us, Shepherd of the soul, to run to You,
our refuge and strength,
our very present help in trouble.

We confess that we have lost sight of the true You
and have been led astray by the phantom of our fears.
Expecting the worst, we have forgotten that You are our
      protector.
Change our expectations so that we may look for Your
      goodness
instead of waiting for the other shoe to drop.

Would You radically transform us from people of fear to
      people of courage,

brimming over with Your freely given Spirit?
Would You fill us with an ever-rising hope
until others begin to inquire about the Source of our
        peace?

The way out of fear is through perfect love,
so enlarge our hearts, Oh God,
to more fully comprehend just how deeply You love us.

Fill us with earnest, growing devotion
until we are fearless in the fear of You.
Turn our worry into wonder
as we seek out Your Scriptures for truth.
Blow on the embers of our faith
until it burns away the husks of our fearful selves,
igniting the spirit of power, love, and self-control within us.

Obedience to unnamable fear is a vestige of our former
        selves, crucified with Christ.
But now we are living stones,
startled awake by the intimate breath of Your Spirit.
Now we are reborn
and belong to You as cherished children.
Now we know love,
and there is nothing left to fear.

Help us to live fully in the peace that You have given us,
for You set us free from our deepest dread.
Help us to laugh at the days to come,
for You secure our every step.
Help us to fear not,

for You are with us.

Help us to swiftly abandon dismay,

for You are our God.

Help us to look for reflections of Your goodness,

for Your triumphant right hand holds us up.

We will not look for death where You have proclaimed life,

but we will take heart,

for the almighty God has already overcome the world.

Amen.

Psalm 27; 46:1; 136 • Proverbs 3:1–8; 29:25; 31:25–26 • Isaiah 41:10–14 • Zephaniah 3:17 • John 16:33 • 2 Corinthians 5 • Galatians 2:20 • Ephesians 2; 5:1–21 • 2 Timothy 1:7 • 1 Peter 2:5; 3:8–22 • 1 John 4

A Liturgy for the Morning
After a Bad Decision

Oh God, we cannot undo what has been done.

Before we even open our eyes,
the weighty companion of regret joins us in bed,
bringing with it reminders of what happened the night
        before—
    the midnight binge over the sink,
    the one-night stand,
    the one drink leading to another until we've lost count.

This morning, we are viscerally reminded that we have no
        life apart from You.
We do not understand why we do what we do
and are frightened to admit that we are not always good.
Would You search our hearts and discern our ways?
Would You restore us and lead us to Your everlasting life?

You, Oh Christ, see our humanity.
You remember that we are made of dust.
You are acquainted with all our ways.
You died to set us free from recklessness
and clothed us in Your righteousness.
We do not stand condemned but loved.

In view of our brokenness, we repent.
With contrite hearts, we settle into the safety of Your love.
Let us spend the whole day and night here.

Where we lack willpower,
    may we surrender to Your Spirit.
Where we lack trust in ourselves,
    may we learn to trust You.
Where we lack restraint,
    may we cultivate patience.

Oh God of infinite chances,
may our first thought in the morning be of Your love
        instead of our shame.
May we continuously return to the shelter of Your wings
and ask for forgiveness when we have done wrong.
May we grieve the painful consequences our choices have
        set in motion
and entrust their outcomes to You.
May we embrace dispositions of humility,
knowing that You have washed our once-scarlet sins as
        white as snow.
May we step into today knowing that we are loved
regardless of how foolish we feel.

May we abound with compassion for those around us,
for we are all living with the consequences of our decisions.

You do not want our attempts at perfection
or our empty promises to do better.
We cannot earn Your approval
or please You with our good behavior.
You simply ask us to return with childlike hearts to You
so that You may comfort us and
restore us to the Father's love.

Amen.

Psalm 5:3; 30; 51; 53:1–3; 77; 91:4; 103:14; 139 • Isaiah 1:18; 53:6; 61:10 • Jeremiah 17:7 • Joel 2:12 • John 3:17; 15:5 • Romans 7:13–8:1 • 2 Corinthians 5:21 • Philippians 2:5–8, 12–13 • Colossians 3:12 • 1 John 1:9

A Liturgy for Those
Consumed by Media

Amid the glowing screens
and talking heads
and blaring headlines
and laymen-turned-experts,
our hearts grow weary and our fingers turn sore
as we refresh our feeds, scrolling to quell the swelling tide
rising within, threatening to topple and overwhelm.

Liberate us, Oh God, from our gluttonous tendencies to
        hoard knowledge
and feast upon information as if it is our daily bread.
Remind us, Oh Father, that our screens are but clouded
        mirrors.
Sift the important news meant to equip us for movement
        and compassion
from the distorted facts and fearmongering headlines

designed only to divide us and destroy the hope we have in
     You.
Keep us from banging our gongs and clanging our
     cymbals.
If we post with the tongues of men and angels but have
     not love,
help us to log out.

Oh Loving God, You see the gravity with which the
     world's suffering pulls us inward.
Extend us grace to grieve for the broken world You adore,
then wash our faces and turn, clear-eyed, to our windows,
through which we can see the trees still clapping,
the sparrows still flying,
the stones still crying out praise to You.

Grant us wisdom to discern what You deem true
and right
and noble
and pure
and praiseworthy
and lovely,
and give us grace to share accordingly.

Amen.

Isaiah 55:12 • Matthew 6:9–13 • Luke 19:40 • John 10:10 • Romans 16:17–19 • 1
Corinthians 13:1–3, 12 • Philippians 4:8

A Liturgy for the Unfaithful

Oh Lord, we are adulterers who have wandered from Your
    love.
We inherited a world that began with teeth sunk into
    fruit—
the garden of a violated covenant—
so it is no wonder our promise-breaking comes as naturally
    as breath.

In ways both big and small, we leave the One who loves us:
    in the morning when we first reach for our phones,
    when our checklists become more pressing than Your
       voice,
    when food is more enticing than Your presence,
    when we cherish earthly relationships more than You.
How quickly we discard the sacred mystery of union with
    You.

These bodies of death know how to leave but forget how
        to stay.

Falsely we have believed that faithfulness to You is a white-
        knuckle effort,

a surplus of *lack*.

Oh Perfect Lover, teach us the wild passion of fidelity.

Reveal the mysterious splendor of Your jealousy.

Remind us that death to self is a resurrection elsewhere.

Oh God, even in my unfaithfulness,

condemnation never escapes Your mouth.

Like the woman caught and surrounded by stones, I am
        met with a gaze of love,

a quiet calling to come home to the One who will wait up
        for me.

Oh Jesus, You desire faithful love and not sacrifice.

You are the bridegroom who rejoices at my coming,

the shepherd who traces my wandering steps,

the father who runs to hold my mud-soaked body to Yours.

Grant me the grace to return freely and fully to You.

Amen.

Genesis 3 • Proverbs 5:3; 6:27–28 • Song of Solomon 8:6 • Isaiah 62:5 • Jeremiah 13:27 • Hosea 6:6; 11:7 • Luke 15:3–7, 11–32 • John 8:1–11; 12:24 • Romans 7:24; 8:1

Acknowledgments

We are filled with gratitude for the communities that have surrounded us, supported us, and strengthened us during the creation of *Liturgies for Hope.*

To our Church of the City New York family: You have encouraged and strengthened us time and again, bolstering our faith with yours. It is an honor to stumble toward God together. It is an honor to be pursued by Him together. It is an honor to wonder at His love together. Jon Tyson, Isaac Gay, Corinne Caraway, and Charissa Pereira: Thank you for your personal investments not only in us and our work but also in the arts community of New York City. In you we have found brothers and sisters who long for beauty and excellence. To be standing on common ground with you is a gift.

Christen Smith, Chris Lo, and Jeff Woldan: You took our humble drafts and gave them a home. Christen, thank you for leading the Church of the City Creative Team with such humility and grace, for recognizing the power of words to bring healing and comfort to people during such a tumultuous time. Chris, your magical design skills stunned us. The online home to our first set of liturgies has a special place in our hearts, and this cover is inspired by your original design. Jeff, thank you for your website-building wizardry and for literally bringing color to these words.

Elizabeth Neep, you believed these liturgies could be a book before we did. Thank you for your persistence, encouragement, and vision. Ashley Hong—you joyful and wonderful person—thank you for enthusiastically connecting us with our agent. This journey to publication would never have happened without either of you.

Chris Park, we could not have asked for a better agent, advocate, friend, cheerleader, and mentor. We are honored to have you guiding us through the publishing process and beyond.

Becky Nesbitt, how did we get so lucky to have you as our editor? Not only did you help us shape this book, but you also brought light and warmth to the process, turning it into a joyful endeavor. Thank you for being a true champion of collaboration and for protecting our voices as debut authors.

To the team at WaterBrook—Ginia Hairston Croker, Johanna Inwood, Chelsea Woodward, Sarah Horgan, Maggie Hart, Elizabeth Eno, Kayla Fenstermaker, Abby DeBenedittis—thank you for your support and enthusiasm from the very beginning, and for making this book a reality.

Kiana, Emalyn, and Alexa—our core, our flames—you have been there in the nitty-gritty. You have cheered us on and gotten up far too early to pray for this book. May we never give up on our longings. May we be persistent women of prayer.

To my (Elizabeth's) family: Thank you to Matthew, Haven, Michael, Annie, John David, and Alli for your support and love. I am blessed beyond belief to have such a wonderful home team. Thank you to Lily, Hudson, David, and future Baby Moore for the joy you bring to our family. To my sweet, encouraging mom and my wise, steadfast dad—thank you for reading and listening, for offering advice and encouragement, for being there in the trenches of the messy and beautiful process of writing. You saw the gift of words in me long before I did. To Ashton, Milly, Hallie, Katie Rose, Hailey, Shauna, and the many other friends who have written with me—thank you. You keep me writing.

I (Audrey) know my portion of this book exists because of the way my family has loved me: Mom and Dad, who will always feel like home; Seth; Ellen; Honey; Poppa; Grandma; Grandpa; Aunt Deidra; Uncle Scott; Lauren; Abigail; Hope; Aunt Kay; Uncle Larry; Drew; Laura; Charity; Aunt Kathy; Uncle Steven. And to my friends, my soulmates, with special thanks to Emily, Carlos, Elizabeth, Kristen, Liz, Renee, Chantal, and Erica, whose support buoyed me in different ways.

Finally, our greatest thanks and awe to the Word, our dearest confidant and friend, and the Spirit, who interceded with the words we did not have.

About the Authors

Audrey Elledge is a graduate of Baylor University and Vanderbilt University and now lives in New York, where she serves at Church of the City New York. Audrey works as a SparkNotes editor, has won the Academy of American Poets Prize and the Virginia Beall Ball Prize, and has been published in *Fathom*.

Elizabeth Moore is a graduate of Mississippi College and the Columbia Publishing Course at Oxford University. Born and raised in Louisiana, she now lives in New York, where she works at Penguin Random House and serves at Church of the City New York. Elizabeth has contributed articles to *Timshel, Transformed, Windrose, Belong,* and *Portico* magazines.